Irrigation Potential in Agriculture of Assam

About the Author

Dr. Mrinal Kanti Dutta (b. 1969) is presently an Associate Professor in Economics in the Department of Humanities and Social Sciences, Indian Institute of Technology Guwahati, Assam. A 1st class Graduate in Economics from Gauhati University, Dr. Dutta was a Gold Medalist from the same university for topping the list of successful candidates in M.A. Examination. He received his Doctorate degree from Gauhati University in 2003. His areas of interest are Agricultural Economics, Environmental Economics, Microeconomics and Econometrics.

Dr. Dutta started his teaching career in 1994 and served in Mangaldai College and Dibrugarh University (Assam) before joining the Department of Humanities and Social Sciences in Indian Institute of Technology Guwahati in 2003.

A number of research scholars have worked/are working under his supervision for their doctoral degree. More than a dozen of his articles have already been published in various journals and edited books in India and abroad. A member of various professional bodies of Economics in India and abroad. Dr. Dutta is also engaged in contributing to various magazines and newspapers on contemporary economic issues.

Irrigation Potential in Agriculture of Assam

Mrinal Kanti Dutta

CONCEPT PUBLISHING COMPANY PVT. LTD.
NEW DELHI-110059

The publication was financially supported by the ICSSR. The responsibility for the facts stated, opinions expressed or conclusions reached is entirely that of the author and the ICSSR accepts no responsibility for them.

The work was evaluated by Professor R. Parthasarthy, CEPT, University of Ahmedabad on behalf of the ICSSR.

ISBN-13 : 978-81-8069-775-3

First Published 2011

Published and Printed by

Concept
Since 1974

Concept Publishing Company Pvt. Ltd.
Regd. Office :
A/15-16, Commercial Block, Mohan Garden
New Delhi-110059 (India)
Phones : 25351460, 25351794, *Fax* : 091-11-25357109
Email : publishing@conceptpub.com
Website : www.conceptpub.com

Editorial Office :
H-13, Bali Nagar, New Delhi-110 015, India

Cataloging in Publication Data--*Courtesy:* D.K. Agencies (P) Ltd. <docinfo@dkagencies.com>

Dutta, Mrinal Kanti, 1969-
Irrigation potential in agriculture of Assam / Mrinal Kanti Dutta.
p. cm.
Revision of the author's thesis (Ph. D.—Gauhati University, 2003) under the title: Problems and prospects of utilisation of irrigation potential in agriculture of Assam.
Includes bibliographical references (p.) and index.
ISBN 9788180697753

1. Irrigation—India—Assam. 2. Irrigation—Government policy—India—Assam. 3. Irrigation efficiency—India—Assam. 4. Agricultural productivity— India Assam. I. Title. II. Title: Problems and prospects of utilisation of irrigation potential in agriculture of Assam.

DDC 333.9130954162 22

Preface

This book is a revised and updated version of my doctoral theiss on "Problems and Prospects of Utilisation of lrrigation Potential in Agriculture of Assam." The study was induced by the problems of agriculture in rain fed areas of Eastern India where resources for agricultural development are in abundance but the returns to labour and capital are low. Assam in Eastern part of India is endowed with huge amount of both surface and ground water reserve, but irrigation infrastructure in the state has remained weak, which has been identified by researchers as one of the principal factors restricting farmers in the state from fuller utilization of the potentials of the 'green revolution' technology. While call for strengthening of irrigation infrastructure is a logical capacity remained underutilized for years together. This discovery induced me to investigate whether demand for irrigation is indeed low among farmers in Assam or shortcomings in the delivery from government owned irrigation facilities account for such poor utilization of existing irrigation capacity.

While carrying out the work, I received help and support from a number of individuals and organizations without which it would have been difficult to successfully complete my work. In carrying out the fieldwork, I received full cooperation from all the 172 sample farmers who patiently responded to my rather long list of questons. The Statistical Call, lrrigation Department, Government of Assam gave me access to all such data which were relevant for my study.

The offices of the Departments of Irrigation and Agriculture in Dibrugarh, Nagaon and Barpeta Districts of Assam provided useful background information for my fieldwork. Regular guidance and advice from my supervisor Professor M.P. Bezbaruah of Gauhati University was crucial in shaping my understanding of the issues and streamlining my analysis of the collected research material. Despite his busy and hectic schedule, he could find out time to attend to a variety of challenges posed by the study. Support from the Indian Council of Social Science Research (ICSSR), New Delhi at various stages was invaluable. The Council provided me with a travel grant for library visit in the early part of my work, a short term fellowship which enabled me to channel my time to the work in an undivided way in the final stage of my research, and the publication grant that has facilitated bringing out of my work in the form of this book. The comments of the ICSSR referee Prof. R. Parthasarathy were very useful and his suggestions have been incorporated to the extent possible while revising and updating the thesis for the book. It is an occasion for me to gratefully acknowledge the support I received from all these individuals and organizations while pursuing my research and publishing the output in the present form. I would also like to put in record my thanks to my wife Kakoli and sons Kingshuk and Krishanu, who gave up some of their due time from me for enabling me to complete this project. Finally, I extend my thanks to Mr. A. K. Mittal of Concept Publishing Company Pvt. Ltd., New Delhi for agreeing to publish the book.

Mrinal Kanti Dutta

Contents

List of Tables

List of Maps

1

Introduction

1.1 Background of the Study

Assam is basically an agrarian economy in the sense that about 69 per cent of the workforce is employed in agriculture sector alone. In 2006-07, this sector contributed about 26 per cent to the Net State Domestic Product of the State (Government of Assam, 2007). The development of the state's economy is dependent, to a large extent, on the development of this sector. But in spite of its overwhelming dominance in the state's economy, the progress of agriculture in the state is far from satisfactory. Agricultural productivity in the state is one of the lowest in the country. For example, the yield rate of rice, the major food crop in the state, stood at 15.41 quintal per hectare in 2005-06 against 37.00 quintal per hectare in Punjab, 30.00 quintal per hectare in Haryana, 29.39 quintal per hectare in Andhra Pradesh, 26.50 quintal per hectare in Tamil Nadu and 20.74 quintal per hectare at all-India level (CMIE, 2007). In view of the relatively higher growth rate of population of the state, for attaining self-sufficiency in food production it will be necessary to achieve a much higher growth rate of agricultural production in the coming years.

The most crucial input for agricultural production is land, the supply of which is inelastic in nature. In view of the high and rising density of population in the state, the pressure on land for agricultural as well as non-agricultural purposes has been going up continuously. As a result, the scope for increasing net area under cultivation has become extremely limited. Higher agricultural growth, has therefore, to come about mainly through more intensive use of the land area under cultivation. This makes the role of irrigation in agriculture very crucial.

Irrigation has been considered as a prime factor for growth of agricultural production for the country as a whole. Due emphasis had, therefore, been given to this important sector even during the British period (Mitra, 1984). The role of irrigation in the field of agriculture is two-fold. On one hand, it promotes growth in agricultural productivity and on the other hand, it contributes towards stabilization of agricultural production. Irrigation imparts stability to agricultural production by reducing farmer's dependence on rainfall, which could be quite uncertain at times. Its contribution to enhancement of agricultural production can come through in a number of ways. As Dhawan (1996) points out, irrigation increases crop output through a rise in (a) proportion of net sown area of a holding and (b) gross cropped area and cropping intensity. It also enhances agricultural productivity directly through yield effects. Apart from these, irrigation helps replacing low-valued crops by high-valued ones which ultimately results in enhancement of the value of agricultural production. The concept of multiple cropping has received much more importance particularly after Green Revolution started in Indian agriculture during the late 1960s. The increasing use of high yielding variety (HYV) for enhancing agricultural output has also necessitated the expansion of irrigation network. HYV possesses high potential. To use it, soil should contain nutrients, which is provided by chemical fertilizer. HYV with chemical nutrients can give the best possible result under irrigated condition only.

Irrigation has a particularly important role in stabilizing

agriculture in a state like Assam. Although the state receives good rainfall almost every year, it is not evenly distributed over time and space. The erratic nature of rainfall makes *kharif* crops vulnerable to the twin problems of flood and drought thereby adversely affecting agricultural productivity. Thus, it has become necessary to expand the area under and output of *rabi* crops which requires adequate and assured irrigation water. The importance of irrigation in the state, thus, arises from the need to stabilize and step up the quantum of agricultural output, to generate income and employment in the rural sector and to meet the mounting food demands of the fast growing population (Sharma, 1992).

However, the scenario of irrigation in the state is paradoxical. The state can boast of a huge amount of surface as well as ground water resources. But these are yet to be fully exploited. In case of created potential also, there exists a huge gap between capacity created and capacity utilised. As per data available, out of a total of 27,06,000 hectares net sown area, only 6.20 per cent is irrigated in 2003-04 (CMIE, 2007) as against 39.11 per cent of net sown area being irrigated for the whole of the country. Interestingly, the figure has been on the decline from 1999-2000 onwards. On the utilisation front also, out of a total created potential of 5,35,212 hectares under government sector in 2005-06 only 60,762.37 hectares were utilised thereby putting the utilisation percentage at as low as 11.35 per cent. Thus while the capacity created under the existing projects do not add up to even a quarter of the cultivated area, the low utilisation of the created capacity is a matter of serious concern. It is, in this context, identifying the factors responsible for low overall utilisation of created irrigation potential in the state becomes important. The studies carried out on the subject so far, although not sufficient to comprehensively cover all the aspects of the problem, have pointed out a number of interesting factors hindering full utilisation of irrigation potential created.

According to Das (1984), this low utilisation is basically

due to the fact that "the aspect of 'Command Area Development', which includes construction of field channels, consolidation of holdings, land levelling and shaping and other infrastructural development had not been planned earlier."

Bezbaruah (1994) attributes the problem of under-utilisation partly to inadequate planning and lack of coordination among various agencies responsible for implementation of irrigation programmes of the state. He, however, is of the view that without a comprehensive study on the subject, it is difficult to point out all the factors responsible for low utilisation rate of irrigation potential created.

The limitations of the above studies in this context are that these studies are basically on agriculture in the state in general and, therefore, have not adequately analysed the problems of the irrigation sector. There are, however, a few studies, which have specifically taken up the issues of irrigation and problem of underutilisation of irrigation potential.

In a study undertaken in Jorhat district of the state, Gohain and Gogoi (1986) found that underutilisation of irrigation arose as a result of interplay of various constraints at farm level. These include prevalence of monocropping system among large farmers, resource constraints among small and marginal farmers, slow development of irrigation distribution network, lack of training and extension programmes to the farmers, non-availability of infrastructural facilities like quality seed and fertilizer in time, institutional credit, etc.

According to Gogoi (1989), frequent breakdowns of the wells, irregular supply of electricity in case of deep tube-wells, lack of proper time schedule for raising different crops in case of surface flow schemes are some of the factors hindering full utilisation of irrigation potential created. He also found that inadequate agricultural extension facilities and lack of coordination among various departments in the development of irrigation in the sample district were also responsible for underutilisation of created irrigation potential.

In a study on Jamuna Irrigation Project of the state, Saikia and Borah (1993) found that non-utilisation of created capacity is due to the poor canal system leading to non-availability of irrigation at the time of requirement, poor project management, loss of water in the process of conveyance and distribution, lack of consolidation of holdings and land development, inadequate agricultural support programme, etc.

The findings of all these studies are very interesting. But these cannot be generalised as the factors for low utilisation of potential created for the state as a whole since these studies are specific to either a project or a location only. As such, to identify the factors responsible for low utilisation of irrigation potential in different irrigation projects in the state, a specific study was considered necessary. It is in this context that the present study was undertaken to examine the performance of the irrigation projects in the state in terms of capacity created and utilised and to identify the factors responsible for low utilisation of the capacity created.

1.2 Objectives

The specific objectives of the study were as follows :

(i) To examine the factors responsible for under-utilisation of created potential of irrigation projects.

(ii) To examine the relative efficiency and effectiveness of different types of irrigation projects in Assam. The efficiencies have been studied with respect to the rate of utilisation of different forms of irrigation in Assam while effectiveness is studied mainly with respect to its capacity to induce the farmers using irrigation to adopt modern inputs such as fertilizer, HYV, etc.

(iii) To suggest policy measures for better utilisation of created irrigation potential and outline the direction for future expansion of irrigation infrastructure in the state .

1.3 Hypotheses

Based on preliminary scrutiny of literature and statistics, the following hypotheses were taken up for verification during the course of the study :

1. Inefficient management of government owned and operated irrigation schemes is responsible for dismal utilisation rate of created irrigation potential in the state.
2. Faulty design has resulted in low utilisation of capacity of the projects.
3. Low utilisation is due to absence of land reform and preparation measures such as consolidation of holdings, levelling of land, etc.

1.4 Data Base and Methodology

The study is based on both secondary and primary data. Secondary data were collected from the publications of various organisations, viz. Directorate of Economics and Statistics, Government of Assam; Irrigation Department, Government of Assam; CMIE report as well as research publications of individual and institutions like Agro-Economic Research Centre for North Eastern Region. The overall picture emerging from the analysis of such secondary data provided the general outlook for a more detailed and intensive investigation of the problems in the field study.

In view of the technical, institutional and sizewise heterogeneity of irrigation projects in the state, the fieldwork had various layers. For major and medium size irrigation projects, 2 out of the 19 existing projects were selected for detailed case study. This selection was made on the basis of preliminary scrutiny of all the projects in the category. The inputs for case study came from the initial project report, reports on the functioning of the project, interview of the officials and a survey of the farmers in the command area. While the reports provided valuable information and insight, the interview of the project officials was necessary for verification and better understanding of the working of the project. The survey of the farmers in the command area helped in cross-checking and also in gathering additional information regarding the problems of utilisation and effectiveness of the project. For selecting the sample of farm households, a two-stage random sampling was used. In the first stage, one village each from different reaches of the major and medium schemes was selected. In the second stage, about 12 per cent of farm households in each selected village were taken at random for collection of data on different aspects of farm operations and use of irrigation water.

Minor irrigation schemes are not homogeneous in nature. On the basis of ownership pattern, these can be classified as government owned or privately owned. From the technical point of view, the government schemes are relatively bigger. These are either surface lift irrigation schemes from river flow or deep tube-well based irrigation schemes. In both these types water is distributed to farmers' fields through canals as in the major and medium schemes. Five schemes from the two districts of Dibrugarh in Upper Assam and Barpeta in Lower Assam were selected for analysis. The methodology adopted for data collection was more or less same as in the case of major and medium schemes. The privately owned schemes are based on shallow tube-wells with maximum command area of two hectares each. For comparability, the sample of farm households under privately owned schemes has been drawn from the same three districts, viz. Dibrugarh, Nagaon and Barpeta, to which the government owned schemes studied belong. The sample of farms was selected using a multi-stage sampling process. In the first stage, two representative Agricultural Extension Officers (AEO) circles were selected from the three districts. Then one representative village from each of the selected circles was taken. Finally, from each of the selected villages about 12 per cent of farm households were selected at random.

Besides using simple statistical tools like averages, ratios and percentages for summarization and comparison, detailed case studies of different schemes have been carried out for identification of factors responsible for the observed utilisation rates under different types of schemes. For further validation of some of the findings regression analysis has also been used.

1.5 Layout of the Book

The Book is comprised of 8 chapters including the present one.

Based on the survey of available literature, chapter two deals with the conceptual issues of irrigation. It also presents a theoretical discussion on the issues relating to the development of irrigation in a state. It covers a variety of issues ranging from the definition of irrigation to utilisation of irrigation potential created. The chapter is also the product of a survey of available literature on irrigation. The findings of some of the empirical works found relevant in the context of the present study have also been summarised in this chapter.

The core of the study begins with chapter three on Irrigation in the Agricultural Economy of Assam. Here a brief description of the structure of agriculture in Assam is followed by an analysis of the trends in the development of irrigation in the state. A comparative study of the development of irrigation at the state level and national level is also presented in this chapter. The chapter ends with identifying the emerging issues for fieldwork. The analysis of secondary data on irrigation in Assam and the findings of the pioneering works on irrigation lead us to certain issues which need further investigation by way of collection of primary data on these issues. The issues that will be dealt with rigorously in the field studies are identified in this chapter.

The four chapters from chapter four to chapter seven are based on the field surveys carried out as a part of the study. Chapter four outlines the background and methodology of the field survey. It also presents the general profiles of the irrigation projects where field studies were carried out. The last part of this chapter deals with the sample profile and its agrarian structure. Chapter five analyses effectiveness and utilisation of different irrigation schemes across regions with the help of some simple statistical tools like averages, ratios and percentages. Detailed case studies of different schemes were carried out for identification of factors responsible for the observed utilisation rates under different types of schemes which is reported in chapter six. In chapter seven, the detailed econometric analysis of the effectiveness of irrigation of different forms in inducing farmers to use better farming practices has been reported.

In the concluding chapter of the dissertation, findings have been summarised, conclusions have been inferred and on the basis of the findings and conclusions, some policy suggestions have been outlined.

REFERENCES

Bezbaruah, M. P. (1994), *Technological Transformation of Agriculture—A Study from Assam*, Mittal Publications, New Delhi.

Centre for Monitoring Indian Economy Pvt. Ltd. (2007), *Economic Intelligence Service : Agriculture*, April, Mumbai.

Das, Manmohan (1984), *Peasant Agriculture in Assam*, Inter India, New Delhi.

Dhawan, B. D. (1996), *Irrigation in India's Agricultural Development*, Sage Publications, New Delhi.

Gogoi, K. (1989), "Irrigation in Assam" in P. C. Goswami (Ed.) (1989), *Agriculture in Assam*, Assam Institute of Development Studies, Guwahati.

Gohain, D. and Gogoi, K. (1986), *Problems of Under-utilisation of Irrigation Potentials*, Agro Economic Research Centre for N.E. India, Jorhat (Mimeographed).

Government of Assam (2007), *Statistical Hand Book of Assam*, Directorate of Economics and Statistics, Assam, Guwahati.

Mitra, A.K. (1984), "Irrigation Sector Reforms—Issues and Approaches", *Economic and Political Weekly*, March 30.

Saikia, T.N. and Bora, D.R. (1993), *Economic Appraisal of CAD Programmes under Jamuna Irrigation Project in Assam (Part I)*, Agro Economic Research Centre for North-East India, Assam Agricultural University, Jorhat.

Sawant, S.D. (1986), "Irrigation and Water Use" in *Indian Agricultural Development since Independence in Indian Society of Agricultural Economics*, Oxford and IBH.

Sharma, P. (1992), *A Study of Irrigation Development and Its Impact on Foodgrains Production in Assam*, Ph.D. Thesis, Gauhati University.

2

Conceptual Issues and Review of Literature

2.1 Definition and Importance

Irrigation is defined as the process of artificially applying water over crops. "Irrigation is any process, other than natural precipitation, which supplies water to crops, orchards, grass or any other cultivated plants" (Stern, 1979). According to Clark (1970), it is "the application of water by human agency, to assist the growth of crops and grass." In other words, the term does not include the other objects for which man stores and controls the flow of water, that is to say, for household and industrial water supplies, for hydroelectric power, for the provision of navigable channels and also for getting rid of unwanted water, in flood measures and in the draining of swamps and waterlogged land. "These other objects, however, may sometimes share with irrigation the use of works, equipment, water flows and administrative organisation and they, therefore, have an indirect effect on economics of irrigation". For Jha (1984), "Irrigation includes all operations or practices in artificially supplying water to the soil for growing crops. It is a means by which water is conveyed to arid areas from rivers, reservoirs or wells to increase the fertility of land." It is the science of harnessing and controlling various natural resources of water for the benefit of agriculture. Scientific irrigation involves knowledge of the available water supply, its conservation and application to the land, the characteristics and needs of different types of soil and the requirements of various crops to be produced.

Irrigation is identified as the most crucial component of agricultural infrastructure. Coupled with HYV seeds, fertilizer, pesticides and other inputs, irrigation can play a major role in boosting up agricultural production and productivity in an economy. In a country with heavy population pressure on land, agricultural growth depends greatly on increasingly intensive use of land. The HYV-fertilizer technology based strategy for agricultural growth through increase in crop yield and cropping intensity, however, depends critically on irrigation. Without assured water in right quantities at the right time crops cannot flourish and multiple cropping may not be possible.

The role of irrigation in the field of agriculture is two-fold. On one hand, it promotes growth in agricultural productivity and on the other hand, it contributes towards stabilization of agricultural production. Its contribution to enhancement of agricultural production can come through in a number of ways. It can enhance agricultural productivity directly through yield effects. Dhawan (1988) pointed out that irrigation increases crop output through a rise in (a) proportion of net sown area of a holding and (b) gross cropped area and cropping intensity. Apart from these, irrigation helps replacing low-valued crops by high-valued ones, which ultimately results in enhancement of the value of agricultural production. Irrigation imparts stability to agricultural production by reducing farmers' dependence on rainfall, which could be quite uncertain at times. Empirical evidences have shown that the percentage of area under dry season crops has gone up significantly in Assam as a result of irrigation. So the significance of flood-damage-prone crops has also gone down considerably. The increasing use of HYV for enhancing agricultural output has also necessitated the expansion of irrigation network. HYV possesses high potential. To use it soil should contain nutrients, which is provided by chemical fertilizer. HYV with chemical nutrients can give the best possible result under irrigated condition only. Alternatively, availability of irrigation water also promotes adoption of new technology embodied in the use of HYV, fertilizers and plant protection measures coupled with improved water management (Sawant, 1986). Thus, irrigation together with a new technology package significantly enhances the productive capacity of land. In fact, as shown by Swaminathan (1981), the introduction of HYVs of wheat and rice in areas covered with assured irrigation has helped in saving of almost 34.5 million hectares of land by 1979 which would otherwise have been additionally needed to produce the same quantum of production of wheat and rice.

2.2 Related Concepts

2.2.1 Irrigation Water and Irrigated Area

Irrigation water is the quantity of water artificially applied in the process of irrigation and does not include precipitation. The irrigation requirement is the quantity of water exclusive of precipitation that is required for crop production and it includes economically unavoidable waste. Irrigated area is the cropped area to which irrigation water has been applied at least once in a season, irrespective of whether the irrigation is adequate, inadequate or in excess of requirement. The irrigated area does not thus take into account the depth or the frequency of watering.

2.2.2 Net and Gross Irrigated Area

Irrigated area can be classified as the net irrigated area and gross irrigated area. The net irrigated area is the area irrigated during an agricultural year (from 1st July to 30th June of the succeeding year) counting the area only once even if two or more crops are irrigated in different seasons in the same land. Gross irrigated area is the total irrigated area under various crops during the year counting the area irrigated under more than one crop during the same year as many times as the number of crops grown, crops sown mixed being taken as one crop. Thus, the area irrigated more than once can be obtained by deducting the net irrigated area from the gross irrigated area.

2.2.3 Irrigation Ratios and Intensity of Irrigation

These are some of the indicators of irrigation. The crop irrigation ratio is the ratio of area irrigated under the crop to the total area under the same crop expressed as percentage. The net irrigation ratio is the ratio of net area irrigated to the net sown area in a year expressed as a percentage, while the gross irrigation ratio is the corresponding ratio between the gross area irrigated and the gross cropped area in a year. The intensity of irrigated cropping is the ratio of gross area irrigated to the net area irrigated expressed as a percentage, while the intensity of irrigation is the sum total of the area irrigated under different crops in a year expressed as a percentage of culturable command area of a project.

2.2.4 Gross Command Area and Culturable Command Area

The gross command area is the total area covered by an irrigation project including uncultivable area under habitation, roads, tanks, wasteland etc. The culturable command area of an irrigation project is the total command area excluding the unculturable land. Nowadays irrigation projects are classified into major, medium and minor categories on the basis of their capacity to irrigate an area in terms of culturable command area (CCA).

2.2.5 Cropping Pattern and Cropping Intensity

Cropping pattern denotes the number of different crops raised per unit of land in different sequence per unit of time. "Cropping pattern means both the time and space sequence of crops. It includes the identification of the most efficient crops of the region, which is considered a homogeneous soil and climatic belt, the rotation on which the crop fits in and the intensity of cropping. Thus the term cropping pattern is used in a more comprehensive sense. When we talk in terms of cropping pattern for a farmer it will mean even cropping scheme and crop intensity best suited for the farm" (ICAR, 1972, p. 15).

Cropping intensity means the number of crops raised in a particular piece of land in a particular year expressed as a percentage, that is, gross cropped area as percentage of operational holding. Thus,

$$\text{Cropping Intensity} = \frac{\text{Gross Cropped area}}{\text{Operational Holding}} \times 100$$

2.2.6 Irrigation Potential Created and Potential Utilised

For a proper evaluation of the performance of irrigation projects it is necessary to ensure that the scientific methods of assessment of irrigation potential created and its actual utilisation are adopted. It is, therefore, necessary to review the concept and meaning of irrigation potential created in respect of an irrigation system. But a considerable amount of controversy and confusion are associated with the use of these two terms. Since these two terms are used in different connotations carrying different meanings, there is a need to have some clarity about these concepts.

For obtaining uniformity in the definitions of these two terms, Planning Commission came out with a definition which is widely accepted. According to Planning Commission, "Irrigation potential is the gross area that can be irrigated from a project in a design year (1st July to 30th June of the succeeding year) for the projected cropping pattern and assumed water allowance on its full development. The gross irrigated area will be the aggregate of the areas irrigated in different cropping seasons, the areas under two seasonal and perennial crops being counted only once in a year." It has been further explained that before an area is included and reported in 'potential created' it has to be ensured that the water for the area to be reported upon is available and conveyance system up to and including irrigation outlet to serve an area up to 40 hectares in the area is completed.

Thus, theoretically there are three important considerations to declare an area irrigable (potential created) from an irrigation system, and these are : (i) availability of water for the area proposed to be irrigated in each season during the irrigation year, (ii) the availability of conveyance system to carry the water up to the outlet head, and (iii) the adherence to the projected cropping pattern. Given these considerations if the area actually irrigated during the irrigation year is smaller than the area proposed to be irrigated (potential created) then there is a case of underutilisation. It follows from this that whenever underutilisation is reported during an irrigation year it means that that part of the water in storage for irrigation has remained unused. Irrigation utilisation is expressed as a percentage of actual irrigated area to the potential created. It means that given the same cropping pattern, whatever is the percentage of area actually irrigated is also the percentage of water actually used up from the storage for irrigation during the year.

But in actual practice, these conditions, to declare an area irrigable (potential created), are hardly fulfilled and as such utilisation percentages estimated as above give inflated figures. Potential is often declared to have been created without giving any attention to construction of proper distribution network. As such even if adequate water is available in the system, the projected area cannot be brought under irrigation because of inadequate conveyance network. Secondly, water available in the storage in a given year may be much less than what is estimated on the basis of dependability percentage which will lead to smaller area irrigated and hence to lower utilisation percentage. Thirdly, the cropping pattern in the ensuing years might have changed considerably such that the entire potential created cannot be irrigated. Utilisation percentage, thus, would be lower if estimated considering the potential created based on the projected cropping pattern.

Thus, as Mitra has observed, "the conventional way of viewing the extent of utilisation as percentage of potential created based on projected cropping pattern may at times be misleading. For getting a clearer and truer picture of underutilisation, it would be necessary to take into account of the amount of water actually released during the year from the quantity in the storage meant for irrigation in addition to the area actually irrigated" (Mitra, 1987)

Full utilisation of irrigation potential especially under major canal systems, although desirable, is of merely notional importance. Taking its various aspects into account, Wade suggested that about 90 per cent utilisation can be considered good enough (Wade, 1976). However, "at the commencement of water supply from a project partial underutilisation may be tolerated as a transitional problem" (Satpathy, 1984).

2.2.7 Participatory Irrigation Management

In recent years the concept of 'participatory irrigation management (PIM)' has gained importance in view of failure of government mechanism in management of irrigation. It has been felt that involvement of stake holding farmers in management and operation of irrigation schemes can enhance overall efficiency of the system. The term 'Participatory Irrigation Management' refers to the participation of irrigation users, the farmers, in the management of the irrigation system not merely at the tertiary level of management but spanning the entire system. Participation, here, is not construed as mere consultation with farmers. The concept of PIM refers to management by irrigation users at all levels of the system and in all aspects of management. The involvement of farmers can be ensured by forming Water Users Associations in the process of management of irrigation system.

2.2.8 Water Users Associations

A Water Users Association (WUA) is a voluntary, non-governmental, non-profit entity established and managed by a group of farmers located along one or several watercourse canals. Water users consist of farmers, peasants and other owners who combine their financial, material and technical resources to improve the productivity of irrigated farming through equitable distribution of water and efficient use of irrigation and drainage systems. A WUA has its leader and it handles the disputes internally, collects fees from the members and manages the system.

There has been continuous conflict over water among water-users in a water course in many countries due mainly to lack of an organized system of equitable water resources distribution. Non-availability of funds for regular operation and maintenance of irrigation schemes further aggravate the problem particularly in case of government irrigation schemes. Existence of a WUA enables the stake-holding farmers to play an active role in management and distribution of water within a system. It also helps farmers to collectively resolve common water and agricultural problems. Members of WUAs benefit from increased crop yields through more efficient water use.

2.2.9 Pricing of Irrigation Water

One of the issues in irrigation management is the efficient allocation of irrigation water for which pricing is considered as an important parameter. It has been increasingly felt that there should be clear linkages between policy objectives and irrigation pricing methods, and consistency with other activities, investments and projects in the sector. There are mainly two methods of pricing of irrigation— non-volumetric pricing and volumetric pricing.

In non-volumetric method of pricing of water, water rates for irrigation use are levied on the basis of area irrigated and the types of the crops grown separately for *kharif* and *rabi* crops. There is a possibility of excess use of water and wastage in this method of water pricing.

For an efficient use of irrigation water, therefore, methods like volumetric supply and pricing of irrigation water system have been advocated and some states in India initiated action for switching over to this method. In this method, the water charge is collected at a rate of unit volume of water supplied. The method requires—

(a) information on the volume used by each farmer or a defined group of users below the measuring point;
(b) a central water authority or water users' organization to set the price, monitor use and collect fees (Cornish, G. *et al.*, 2004).

In this method the farmer has to pay depending upon his decision regarding the water usages. Thus the rate and the total revenue vary from farmer to farmer, land to land, and also crop to crop, even in the same ayacut thereby creating a scope for financial incentive for his efficiency in water use. Most of the advanced countries advocate for this type of revenue structure. The reason for introduction of volumetric measurement and pricing of irrigation water is to use scared water resources judiciously.

The issues governing the pricing of irrigation water are mainly the following: recovering costs to achieve financial sustainability, limiting demand for water to the environmentally sustainable level and providing a mechanism that facilitates transfer of water use from lower to higher value uses (whether 'value' is financial, economic, social, or whatever). While the first two have their own relevance, the third one is also significant to planners and policy-makers, and can be addressed through tradable water rights.

The most obvious choice for a system to recover costs is an easy-to-implement, non-volumetric method, such as area pricing or output taxation. Area pricing has little or no effect on demand for water by individuals and its effect on water productivity is negligible. Indeed, imposition of high, non-volumetric charges may lead to higher water use as users feel entitled to use as much as they want, as it has been paid for. Volumetric methods are intrinsically unsuited to the recovery of costs, because while the costs of system operation are relatively stable, the revenues from uncertain sales — possibly compounded by uncertain prices — provide an operating agency with limited financial security. Tradable water rights separate the issue of revenue generation (the payment by users for the cost of supplying) from pricing the resource (payments among the holders of water rights for the benefit of use).

Where the objective is to control demand, there are three

options : quotas (which is not a charging mechanism); volumetric charges at levels sufficient to induce the required reduction in demand; or tradable water rights. Volumetric charging is not observed as a mechanism to bring demand and supply into balance — this is better achieved through water allocations (quotas). Volumetric pricing can promote some degree of water conservation. However, at the prices normally applied, their influence on the level of demand expressed is slight.

Historical, topographical, hydrological, and social differences in irrigation projects throughout the world have created many variations of dealing with water as a "volume". In South Asia, irrigation designers and managers typically talk about water in terms of "water duty", which means "flow rate". Perhaps because of the predominance of run-of-the-river systems in many areas of South Asia, managers and designers are not accustomed to thinking about or managing water deliveries volumetrically.

In projects with reservoir supplies, a specific volume is often available for distribution in a season. Therefore, engineers and managers in these types of projects are more inclined to think in terms of unsteady flow, in which flow rates are constantly changed for various periods of time, to make the best use of an available volume of water.

However, as Burt (2007) has observed, volumetric water pricing and allocation cannot be accomplished simply by issuing a decree, changing laws, or forming water user associations. To actually implement a volumetric water pricing system requires the installation of structures such as good measurement devices at turnouts and supply canals, water level control structures in the supply canals, improved communications, changes in management styles, etc. Thorough planning, attention to the details, and ability to enforce rules, greatly improve the programme's chances for success.

2.3 Methods of Irrigation

There are certain scientific methods of irrigation which have been evolved by different countries in the world for efficient use of water to the fields. The irrigation water may be applied to crops by flooding it on the field surface, by applying it beneath the soil, by spraying it under pressure or by applying in drops. The water supply, the types of soil, the topography of the land, the crops to be irrigated determine the correct method of irrigation to be used. The most common methods of irrigation are as follows :

(i) Surface Irrigation Methods,
(ii) Sub-Surface Irrigation Methods,
(iii) Sprinkler Irrigation Methods,
(iv) Drip (Trickler) Irrigation Methods, and
(v) Lift Irrigation Methods.

2.3.1 Surface Irrigation Methods

In such methods water is applied directly to the soil surface from a channel located at the upper reach of the field. Water may be distributed to the crops in border strips, check basins or furrows. It involves the application of water to the land from a ditch or a low-pressure pipe system. Two general requirements of prime importance to obtain high efficiency in surface irrigation methods are properly constructed water distribution systems and on farm development like land levelling, etc. to permit uniform distribution of water over the field.

2.3.2 Sub-Surface Irrigation Methods

In this method water is applied below the ground surface by maintaining an artificial water table at some depth depending upon the soil texture and the depth of the plant roots. Water reaches the plant roots through capillary action. The water application system consists of field supply channels, ditches or trenches suitably spaced to cover the field adequately and drainage a large quantum of good quality water and a sub-soil barrier or a high water table.

2.3.3 Sprinkler Irrigation Methods

The sprinkler irrigation has been considered as the potential method compared to surface irrigation. Because of its many advantages, this mode of irrigation is gaining popularity on food crops, orchards, cotton and vegetables in areas where sprinkler is economically justifiable and technically feasible.

In this type of irrigation, water is sprayed onto the air and allowed to fall on the ground surface like rainfall. The spray is developed by the flow of water under pressure through small nozzles. The pressure is usually obtained by pumping. By adjusting the nozzle pressure of pumping and spacing of the sprinkles, water can be supplied to the plants at a uniform rate to suit the infiltration rate of the soil, thereby obtaining efficient irrigation.

Sprinkler irrigation can be used on all soils except heavy clay soils and for all types of crops except paddy and jute both of which require copious watering. Another advantage of sprinkler irrigation is that land need not be levelled as in other methods of irrigation, and the method is best suited to irregular topography. There are two types of sprinklers. For higher-pressure operation, rotating head type is used, while for low heads, perforated pipes are used. Sprinklers need not be stationary and can be attached to moving machines.

2.3.4 Drip (Trickler) Irrigation Methods

Drip irrigation or Micro Irrigation, as it is popularly known, is the most efficient method of irrigation. Water is applied at low rate over a long period of time, at frequent intervals directly into the plant's root zone and also through a low-pressure delivery system.

Drip irrigation system delivers water to the crop using a network of main lines, sub-mains and laterals with emission points spaced along their lengths. Each emitter or orifice supplies a small, precisely controlled, uniform application of water, nutrients and other required growth substances directly into the root zone of the plant. Water and nutrients enter the soil from the emitter, moving into the root zone of the plant through the combined forces of gravity and capillarity. In this way, the plant withdraws moisture and nutrients and replenishes almost immediately, ensuring that the plant never suffers from water stress, thus enhancing quality, its ability to achieve growth and high yields.

The drip method of irrigation has been found to be very useful in reclaiming and developing the desert area. Experiments on a number of crops like tomato, cucumber, muskmelon, pepper, sweet, corn etc. showed that in all cases the yield under drip irrigation far exceeded those under sprinkler or furrow irrigation, and in some cases, the yields were more than double, even though the quantity of water applied to any particular crop was, more or less, the same for all the irrigation methods (Jha, 1984).

This method reduces salt concentration in the root zone when irrigated with poor quality ground water. Like the sprinkler method drip irrigation permits the application of fertilizer through the system. Compared to surface and sprinkler method, drip irrigation can achieve a 90 per cent or more application efficiency. But the main disadvantages of the system include the high initial cost, possibility of building up soil salinity if poor quality water is used continuously, less durability, etc.

2.3.5 Lift Irrigation Methods

This system of irrigation is now being increasingly used in India. Due to the development of high head pumps there is a new opportunity for irrigating high lands. A lift is an installation of pump, at a height close to the riverbank that taps water from the river and allows it to reach the field through small channels constructed for this purpose. Lift irrigation may be of two types : (a) surface lift and (b) ground water lift. In case of surface lift irrigation systems, water is lifted from rivers or rivulets with the help of a pump placed at a barge on the river or rivulet. In case of ground water lift, water is lifted through deep or shallow tube-wells depending on the depth of the well. While deep tube-wells tap deep seated aquifers (more than 300 feet deep from the earth's surface), the shallow tube-wells tap shallow aquifers (less than 200 feet from the earth's surface).

A lift irrigation project can handle much larger areas than a tube-well and should be adopted wherever facilities exist. The lift method is extensively used in many countries of the world, the lift going up to 1000 metre in some cases.

2.4 Size Classification of Irrigation Works

Another classification of irrigation works, peculiar to India, is on the basis of the size of the schemes. Thus, irrigation works are classified into three categories, viz. minor irrigation, medium irrigation and major irrigation. This three-way classification was evolved during the British times, and was linked to the quantum of capital resources required for executing irrigation works of varying scale and size. This procedure was followed by Indian planners up to 1978. Initially, the attempt was to classify irrigation works according to mode of financing. They were divided into two main classes — productive and minor. Productive works were those whose construction was wholly or mainly financed from loans. Minor works were those in which the cost was charged to the general revenues.

At the time of setting up of the First Irrigation Commission in 1901, there were three main classes of irrigation works — (i) productive, (ii) protective, and (iii) minor works. Protective works were those works, which were not likely to fulfil the conditions of a productive work, but which had been sanctioned against the famine fund on the ground of their protective value. The First Irrigation Commission proposed a simplification in the classification of irrigation works. Its proposals were as follows :

(i) *Major Works* : Works which were to include all works for which reliable capital and revenue accounts were kept, whether the capital cost was met from loan funds or from the famine grant or from current revenues.

(ii) Minor Works : Works which were to include all works for which capital accounts were not kept. These were sub-classified into (a) minor works for which revenue accounts were kept, and (b) minor works for which revenue accounts were not kept.

With the advent of the planning era in India, we had one more class of irrigation works, viz. 'medium' between major and minor irrigation projects. The medium irrigation projects were those projects the cost of which was more than Rs. 10 lakh but less than Rs. 500 lakh. Thus we had three classes of irrigation works, viz., major, medium and minor.

The financial yardstick applied to irrigation scheme constructed long ago was not found practicable, on account of the change in prices. In 1959, it was decided that pre-plan schemes irrigating up to 1600 hectares should be regarded as Minor schemes. The financial ceiling of Rs. 10 lakh for individual minor irrigation schemes was later raised to Rs. 15 lakh and has further been revised upward, from 1970 to Rs. 25 lakh in the plain areas and to Rs. 30 lakh in hill areas. The criteria earlier used for classification of irrigation works were revised from 1978-79 with specification of technical norms rather than financial norms, uniformly for all the three categories. The categorization of the schemes is now based on their culturable command areas (CCA). Both these definitions are given in Table 2.1.

Table 2.1 : Criteria for Classification of Irrigation Schemes

Category	*Old Criteria*	*New Criteria*
(1)	*(2)*	*(3)*
Minor Schemes	Cost up to Rs. 25 lakhs in plain areas and up to Rs.30 lakh in hill areas	Those with CCA up to 2000 hectares
Medium Schemes	Other than minor irrigation schemes with CCA up to 10,000 hectares	Those with CCA above 2,000 hectares and up to 10,000 hectares
Major Schemes	With a CCA of more than 10,000 hectares	Those with a CCA of more than 10,000 hectares

Source : Swaminathan (1981) Table 4, p.3.

The classification of irrigation works to major, medium and minor schemes is not a satisfactory usage for a number of economists. It is because of the fact that in our irrigation history, the area benefiting from minor irrigation works (dug-wells, tube-wells, tanks, etc.) has always exceeded the corresponding area covered by major and medium irrigation works, mostly comprising canals originating from big dams and barrages built across rivers (Dhawan, 1997). Thus, the literal connotation of 'minor' can be quite misleading in as much as it does not reflect the great importance of small scale works in the Indian irrigation sector.

2.5 Review of Literature

For any scientific investigation past experience strengthens the base of the researcher. Therefore, review of literature is a prerequisite for any scientific investigation. In this section, keeping the objectives of the present study in view, a review of the available research studies compiled from both published and unpublished reports has been made under the following sub-heads :

(i) Impact of Irrigation on Yield, Cropping Pattern, Employment, etc.
(ii) Irrigation Management.
(iii) Underutilisation of Irrigation Potential and Related Aspects of Irrigation Economics.
(iv) Relative Efficiency of Different Forms.
(v) Minor Irrigation Schemes.

2.5.1 Impact of Irrigation on Yield, Cropping Pattern, Employment, etc.

D.R. Gadgil's (1948) work evaluating economic effects of irrigation with reference to Godavari and Pravara canal throws light on many direct and indirect benefits of irrigation. It concludes that provision of irrigation facility to the people coming under these two canal command areas has enabled them to have a superior cropping pattern, higher per acre productivity and higher gross farm income.

According to Clark (1970), it is always worthwhile to concentrate irrigation water on the highest valued and heaviest growing crops. However, over-watering not only fails to give any additional yield but also may, if persisted in, have very serious consequences by raising the water table to plant root level and thus make the land unsuitable for cultivation as was observed in large areas of West Pakistan.

Satpathy (1984) opined that the benefit of irrigation had been found to be positive in Orissa. The author studied the major impact of irrigation on development of farm economy and examined the appropriateness of the important policies persuaded for irrigation development for the period of 1951-1981 in the state. He concluded that even though irrigation expansion had not been able to appreciably push up the net sown area in Orissa, the 'acerage effect' of irrigation had been significant with the increase in the index of crop intensity, resulting from double and multiple cropping. The "crop pattern effect" had been favourable in the state and crop substitution had taken place in both *kharif* and *rabi* seasons. The shift of cropping pattern from local variety crops to high yielding variety (HYV) crops had resulted in a rise in yield rate. The author also pointed out that the expansion of irrigation had increased the level of on-farm development.

Dhawan (1988) had made a detailed study on irrigation in India's agricultural development. According to him, an extensive irrigation programme in low and medium rainfall states would greatly assist in reaching the goals of maximising agricultural growth, achieving stability in output and ensuring an equitable sharing of the gains of growth. The author also pointed out that investments in irrigation in high rainfall regions are bound to have low returns in the shape of gains in production and output stability. The protective role of irrigation during drought has also been appraised by the author and found that no single state of India has achieved drought proofing of its agriculture through irrigation.

The study also examined the impact of irrigation on crop yields with reference to different forms of irrigation. It observed that irrigated yield was highest on farms watered by private tube-wells, and lowest on those dependent on tanks, canal irrigation falling in between these two. In low and medium rainfall states of the country, the construction of surface irrigation has tremendously contributed to the quantum of ground water and, hence, to the establishment of privately owned wells. Dhawan noticed such a development particularly in the tail reaches of a canal where the water supply is not as plentiful as in the top end, and the protective canals that are deliberately designed for under-irrigation. The conventional view of superiority of ground water over surface irrigation conveniently overlooks the fact that the latter is a necessary compliment for the development of the former.

Impact of irrigation on intensity of cropping is the central topic of many of the available irrigation literatures. But economists over the years have expressed differing views on it.

Rao, *et al.* (1988) discerns "some evidence of a mild increase in the impact of irrigation on cropping intensity" but Alagh (1987) is concerned at the elasticity of intensity of cropping with irrigation now approaching zero in some states. Satya Sai (1990) found that in Punjab-Haryana region, the impact of irrigation on intensity of cropping during the post-HYV period was lower than that in the pre-HYV period.

Dhawan and Dutta's (1992) study focuses on the measurement aspects of the impact of irrigation on intensity of cropping. It comprised three sections dealing (i) methodology, (ii) temporal results and (iii) cross-section results. Multiple regression technique was used to undertake cross-sectional and time series analysis of impact of irrigation on intensity of cropping. While doing so, they carefully dealt with some methodological issues relating to (i) the very definition of intensity of cropping, especially the issue of its adjustment for the length of the period for which different crops occupy land from the date of their preparatory tillage to final harvesting, (ii) the definition of irrigation variable for multiple regression purpose. Here the two-fold issue is one of choosing between gross and net irrigated area statistics on one hand, and relating to chosen one to either net or gross cropped (sown) area on the other, (iii) the usual specification of the regression model. The study revealed a definite evidence of the close relationship between irrigation development and the rise in intensity of cropping at the all India level. Of course, the cross-sectional study and time series study of the relationship between rise in irrigation and intensity of cropping gave slightly different values of the intensity of cropping. This may be attributed to the omission of variables like tractorisation from the regression model.

Chatterjee's (1995) study covered a number of aspects of

irrigation in the state of West Bengal. It observed that irrigation had conferred its benefits on net sown area, cropping intensity and crop yields. Out of these, intensity of cropping manifested maximum response. As for net sown area the role of irrigation had been complicated by demographic factors. With regard to crop yields, irrigation played a catalytic role by augmenting the use of HYV seeds and fertilizers. According to the author, efficiency of irrigation may be enhanced gradually through realisation of its relationship to other environmental variables, through the consorted use of traditional and modern irrigation systems and also through coordination between various performing sectors. This requires comprehensive planning with equal emphasis being given to surface and ground water resources. In view of the fact that surface water is susceptible to monsoonal fluctuation and due to increasing moribund conditions in the eastern parts, the author suggested to lay more emphasis on ground water irrigation. Stress must also be given on the selective adaptation of technology based upon ecological considerations as well as upon the conjunctive and judicious use of surface and ground water to ensure maximum benefits in the long run.

In a study relating to Punjab, Singh (1991) observed that the use of irrigation in the state induced the farmers to demand hired labour. But this demand varied across farms. In large farms the demand for hired labour tended to decrease. In small farms, the farmers tend to work for a lesser number of hours when irrigation facilities was extended.

In the article "Irrigation and Water Use", Sawant (1986) had discussed at length the impact of irrigation on agriculture. She observes that irrigation not only enhances yield rates of agriculture but also induces farmers to adopt modern technology in the fields thereby raising the capacity of land substantially. It also imparts stability in yields per hectare and thereby reduces fluctuation in production levels. Regarding stability of agriculture, the author, however, observed that "if the supplies of irrigation are highly vulnerable in years of low rainfall, when they are most badly needed — as is observed in the case of a state like Tamil Nadu, they may not induce desired stability in production levels."

Pawar (1989) undertook a study on the relationship between irrigation and agriculture with reference to the upper Krishna Basin of Maharastra. The author observed that, irrigation in association with mechanical and bio-chemical inputs had influenced the land use in the region. The net sown area had also increased. Overall the study area had 66.82 per cent of land under cultivation. This proportion was high (80%) in the eastern parts and low (below 40%) in the western part of the region. Although the entire cropping pattern seems to be governed by agro-climatic conditions, irrigation had played a prominent role by changing the nature and extent of cropping pattern.

A number of studies were undertaken in Assam to assess the impact of irrigation on yield, cropping pattern, employment scenario in the economy. An attempt has been made here to review the available literature on irrigation impact with reference to the state of Assam.

Ali (1975) undertook a study to assess the impact of Mayong Lift Irrigation Project in Nagaon on the cropping pattern of the area. The author found the impact of irrigation project to be encouraging. Normally, farmers raised paddy and jute in the *kharif* season and mustard, pulses, wheat and some other minor crops in the *rabi* season. With the introduction of irrigation there was a change in the crops grown in the area. The traditional *rabi* crops were being replaced by both traditional and HYV paddy. There was considerable increase in the productivity of land for the adoption of irrigation and HYV paddy seeds. The average yield of paddy increased from 15.6 quintals to 21.3 quintals per hectare. The farmers were successfully growing HYV paddy during flood free months with the help of irrigation. The cropping intensity had increased to a great extent. The marginal and small farmers were also benefited. The study also observed a significant change in crop intensity which was about 200 per cent.

Saikia, P. D. and Bora, A.K. (1975) in a study in Nahatia village in Jorhat District found that yield had increased to 2268 kg. per hectare in irrigated fields in 1974 from 1843 kg. per hectare in 1972 under rainfed condition.

Phukan (1985) studied the impact of deep tube-well irrigation of crop production in Jorhat District of Assam and found that till the time of field investigation, there was limited use of the irrigation potential by the farmers. Taking only the sample farmers into consideration, it was found that only 55 per cent of the potential created by the deep tube-wells under study were utilised. Considering the total potential created in the district of Jorhat, proportion of utilised potential could be much lower.

Phukan (1986) undertook a similar study on the impact of deep tube-well on crop production in Kamrup district of Assam to examine the impact of irrigation on (i) cropping pattern, (ii) crop intensity, (iii) yield rates of irrigated crops, and (iv) adoption of improved inputs and practices due to introduction of irrigation. The author observed that the utilisation of irrigation water by the sample farmers was limited to autumn paddy (*ahu*) and wheat cultivation only. The impact of irrigation on crop production was not found to be encouraging. The cropping pattern of the beneficiary sample had shown no significant changes over the non-beneficiary farmers. The intensity of cropping increased only nominally due to irrigation. The extent of double cropped area in the beneficiary sample was 66.75 per cent compared to 48.82 per cent in the non-beneficiary sample.

Gogoi (1993) studied the impact of irrigation on agricultural development in Kamrup district of Assam. She also made a comparative study between the farmers benefited by irrigation schemes and those deprived from these facilities. The author found a positive impact of irrigation on the agricultural development in the district. Even though irrigation was not able to change the cropping pattern of the sample areas appreciably except introduction of high yielding varieties (HYV) of *ahu* rice cultivation in irrigated fields during autumn season, the acerage effect of irrigation had been significant with increase in the index of crop intensity as reflected in double and multiple cropping in the sample areas. The impact of irrigation on yield had too been favourable in the sample areas with average per hectare yields rates of both rice and other crops in irrigated lands. In short, as a cumulative effect of increased crop intensity, adoption of HYV *ahu* rice cultivation and enhanced yield rates of all irrigated crops, there had been an augmentation in the total volume of agricultural production in the sample areas.

2.5.2 Irrigation Management

Sukla and Gurjar (1990) observed that failure of majority of our irrigation projects is not due to lack of technical soundness or economic feasibility, but due to the lack of efficient system of distribution and utilisation of irrigation water. Even the available irrigation water is not applied to the crops at the most appropriate time and in optimal quantities to ensure maximum possible production and efficient use of water. Thus efficient management of the existing irrigation systems is a must for better utilisation of the potential created.

The main system management has been considered a key to better performance of irrigation projects. Chambers (1992) has given top priority to this aspect for better performance of the projects in future. The main system management refers to management of software aspects of the tapping, allocation, scheduling and delivery of water on main systems down to and including outlets and the disposal of water in drains below chaks. It includes planning, decision-making, operation of controls and communications both upward to managers and downward to group of farmers. But the author has remarked that the aspect has not been a subject of much professional attention whereas its potential has been confirmed by research and experience.

Palanisami (1984) considers irrigation water management as a determinant of canal water distribution in India. According to him, performance of canal irrigation has not been at par with the expectation so far. Although tremendous amount of investment has been made towards installation of physical infrastructure, the management aspects of the irrigation systems have not been rightly emphasized, rather neglected. The mounting cost of construction, exhaustion of favourable construction sites and disputes over sharing water rights between neighbouring states constraint the investment in new projects. Palanisami's study was based on the lower Bhavani project of Tamil Nadu. He observed that availability of irrigation water in alternate year led to the investment on private well irrigation within the command areas as the high rate of seepage/percolation of canal water (almost half) tremendously improved ground water availability in the area.

In majority of irrigation projects, tail-end deprivation is a common problem where upper reach farmers take most of the benefits. Deprivation takes many forms, and is reflected in various indicators including water supply, irrigation intensity, cultivation practices, yields and incomes. Hence, allocation of water under different reaches of the canal and among different size of holdings in different seasons needs special attention. Bhingraj (1987) found that top-end farmers had plenty of water, much more than is economically necessary, with the tail-end farmers having hardly any water to irrigate their crops. He opined that this trend not only leads to colossal wastage of water resources but also deprives the tail-end farmers to fully utilise their holding.

Mitra's (1984) study based on Mula Irrigation Project in Maharashtra found that farmers in the head reaches were allowed to take water while the canals further down were under construction. They, therefore, had ample water in this initial period and adopt water intensive cropping pattern. When lower reaches are ready they mount intense resistance to the consequent reduction in their water supply. This has been a particular problem of canal schemes in drought prone areas, where irrigation policy aims to spread water over as large an area as possible. With regard to cropping pattern of the sample farmers it was observed that there was a concentration of heavy water using crops in the upper reaches of the canal, thereby adversely affecting the very aim of irrigation in the drought prone areas, i.e. to spread water over as large an area as possible.

Sukla and Gurjar (1990) found that 60 per cent of the surveyed farmers from the head position of the canal adopted improved crop production technology having improved seed, fertilizer and agricultural machines. The use of inputs decreased to 40 per cent and 20 per cent in the middle and tail-end portions respectively. There is need to consider the subject with a view to increasing technology adoption.

Mitra (1987) again observed that long gestation period in developing full potential of the system because of inadequate planning has led to cost escalation which could have been avoided. A cost benefit exercise carried out for the project shows that extending irrigation over wider area in the canal command by growing seasonal crops instead of sugarcane on more than stipulated area, may not only increase the gross area irrigated, spread over wider area under canal command, but may also improved the benefit-cost ratio of the project. Delay in the construction of distributary network even after full storage had been created not only led to cost escalation but also to a lopsided irrigation development (because distribution network only in the upper reaches of the main canal was completed).

Use of ground water in Indian irrigation scenario has been on the rise, thanks to the development of rapid electrification of pump sets thereby reducing the unit cost of water. But at the same time it has created some adverse impact on water management practices. Bore-well and tube-well have privatised ownership of irrigation, while canals and tanks are being controlled by government. According to Narayanamoorthy (1996), the private ownership of irrigation has induced farmers to use water extravagantly. It has also reduced their participation in irrigation related activities which were governed and controlled by farmers before owning bore-wells. Changes in the tariff policy from the pro-rate (PR) to flat-rate (FR) and free electricity have further weakened farmers' participation in irrigation activities. Narayanamoorthy's paper focuses on the impact of electrification of pump sets and changes in the electricity tariff policies on the use of electricity and management of ground water at three different levels— (i) India as a whole, (ii) the state of Tamil Nadu level, and (iii) field level comparing bore-well and non-bore-well farmers. The study has shown that at the national level, per pump set consumption of electricity has increased substantially, but the increasing rate of ground water area is not appreciable compared to electricity consumption. Consumption of electricity per pump set has not increased significantly after the introduction of PR and FR in Tamil Nadu as in the other states. At the field level, round the clock electricity supply and low cost for water lifting are the two main factors causing mismanagement of water and electricity.

In view of the specific benefits accruing from surface and ground water based projects, a number of economists have laid emphasis on conjunctive use of surface and ground water for better performance of the irrigation sector. The Planning Commission in the Seventh Plan document emphasized the need for joint allocation of surface and ground water. It observes —

"The conjunctive use of surface and ground water would be encouraged in the minor irrigation programmes. Dug-well programmes in the canal command areas would be encouraged under the command area development programmes for supplementing canal irrigation. The conjunctive use programme under the various development sectors would be coordinated so that the existing irrigation facilities are put to the best use and the gestation period of irrigation utilisation under major and medium irrigation schemes is reduced."

Dhawan (1986) has emphasized on the need for conjunctive use of surface and ground water. But he has put a query as to what optimum level of ground water should be made available to back up surface water systems to compensate the inadequacy. The exclusive development of either source of irrigation can prove unproductive in the long run.

Dhawan (1987) again observed that, whenever surface or ground water had been developed in isolation from each other, the experience was consistently bad with regards to resource conservation. Further, exclusive reliance on ground water as a source of irrigation created the problem in a reverse manner.

2.5.3 Underutilisation of Irrigation Potential and Related Aspects of Irrigation Economics

Creating irrigation potential by the major irrigation projects is a costly affair. It requires huge amount of investment to create irrigation potential on a hectare of land. But in spite of massive public investment on the schemes, utilisation of irrigation potential is found to be very low, leaving a wide gap between potential created and its utilisation. Such underutilisation is more marked in the case of major and medium irrigation projects. In view of this, studies on utilisation of irrigation potential assume importance. But interestingly issues relating to utilisation of irrigation potential did not receive much attention till 1980s (Reddy, 1998). Of late, however, a number of economists including Niranjan Pant, K. Palanisami, A.K. Mitra, Robert Wade, Robert Chambers, etc. have undertaken some independent studies on the subject.

Pant's (1981) study is limited to some aspects of irrigation administration of Kosi Project in Bihar. He emphasized on the need for better clarification of the concepts 'potential' and 'utilisation'. According to Pant, mere setting up of an irrigation system is not important. What is required is to evolve an organisational system which can operate it successfully. He attributes the gap in utilisation mainly to inefficient management of water supplies at the system level. According to him, the main constraints affecting the efficiency in utilisation are lack of cooperation among the bureaucracy and beneficiaries, non-completion of residual work, faulty design of outlets and canals, etc.

Mohammed Yousuf (1990) had examined the problem of irrigation potential of Sriramsagar Project in Andhra Pradesh. He found that water released in relation to water requirement diminishes as one moves from head distributary to tail-end distributary. A study of the utilisation of irrigation potential under the distributaries in relation to factors like location, length and ayacut reveals that each one of the factors is inversely related to the level of performance. Precarious water supply position in tail-end reaches has been found to affect adversely not only land utilisation but also yields as compared to farmers in head reaches.

Bhingraj (1987) studied the extent of underutilisation of irrigation resources in India and found that in surface flow irrigation projects underutilisation is a serious problem.

According to Mitra (1991), underutilisation of irrigation

potential is a serious problem mainly in the surface irrigation system in India. But for avoiding differences in estimates of the same, the term 'underutilisation' has to be clearly defined and understood. He emphasized that the present definition of underutilisation based entirely on 'area approach' (area not irrigated as percentage of potential created) was misleading and that along with area actually irrigated it was necessary to take into account the water actually used up from the storage. "Since overirrigation and deviation from assumed cropping pattern are the two main causes of underutilisation and unequal distribution of water over the canal command, the remedy for such malallocation and distribution of available water has to be sought in the design of irrigation network and in the existing system of distribution of water, specially in the water scarce regions of India", he opined.

Easter (1974) studied the Sambalpur Irrigation Project and found that the irrigation potential was not utilised by the farmers in its fullest extent. The study found a poor drainage system in the command area. The author opined that the existing field channels were another important factor responsible for non-utilisation of irrigation water in its created capacity by the farmers of the area.

Dutta and Chang (1986) observed that not only demand side factors but also supply side factors were responsible for the underutilisation of the created irrigated potential in the Sona command area of Bihar. Several attributes of supply like the geographical location of the beneficiary village, timely supply and steadiness of supply from year to year stood as hindrances of the optimum utilisation of irrigation water in the area under study. It was opined that unless these attributes were properly taken care of while supplying irrigation water, huge externality and 'free rider' problems continued to arise. Hence, the authors urged for the development of appropriate collective organisations at inter-village levels and asked for complete overhauling of the government machinery which was in charge of supplying irrigation water.

Srinivasmurthy (1990) has observed that the under-utilisation of the created irrigation potential has been most marked in respect of the major and medium irrigation projects throughout all the plan periods. According to him, this is mainly due to the fact that there has been delay in the construction of the feeder canals and the channels which are required to take water from the main canals to the land. He has suggested a more comprehensive and integrated planning of irrigation projects including construction of feeder canals and the necessary land development works simultaneously with the construction of the reservoirs and the main canals for a better performance of the irrigation projects. Additional created potential also depends on the adaptability of the farmers to the modern methods of farming. This necessitates the timely supply of inputs like fertilizers, hybrid seeds, pesticides and new agricultural implements.

Programme Evaluation Organisation of the Planning Commission (1966) made an attempt to examine the problems of underutilisation of irrigation potential in some of the major irrigation projects in the country. One of the reasons cited for underutilisation of irrigation potential by the study is the definition of irrigation potential currently in use which needs improvement and clarification. According to the study, the area of irrigation potential should be determined after taking into account water requirements of the cropping pattern prescribed by the project authorities. The cropping pattern as preferred by the farmers is not fully allowed for in the calculation of water requirement. If the prescribed pattern endorses light irrigation and the farmers' preferences are for wet crops, then the irrigation potential figures turn out to be overestimates. To that extent, estimates of underutilisation, if any, of the potential becomes unrealistic. The study points out that in determining the irrigation potential, the figures should be built up separately for *rabi* and *kharif* seasons and should be uniformly reported both in gross and net terms. The other factors for under-utilisation, as pointed out by the study, include absence of consolidation of holdings and other land development works, problems of seepage and waterlogging, lack of coordination among different agencies involved in implementation of irrigation programmes, etc. The study also pointed to the problem of tail-end deprivation where farmers in the tail reach do not get sufficient water because of wastage in the upper reaches.

According to Puttaswamaiah (1977), underutilisation of irrigation potential in large scale irrigation projects takes place mainly due to two reasons : (i) In the initial stages, there are no field channels to serve the particular area or enough water supply due to various reasons including breaches in the distributaries and sub-distributaries and the consequent starving of field channels, and (ii) non-completion of other works of land development like levelling and bunding of the area, construction of water distributaries and the necessary roads and paths.

Gohain and Gogoi (1986) undertook a study to examine the problems of underutilisation of irrigation potential in Jorhat district of Assam. They observed that though percentage of irrigated area in the state is quite low, the available water from various irrigation sources is even not utilised properly by the farmers. Underutilisation of irrigation potential arises as a result of the interplay of various constraints at farm level, such as prevailing monocrop system among large farmers, resource constraints among small and marginal farmers, slow development of irrigation distribution system, lack of training and extension programme to the farmers, non-availability of infrastructural facilities like quality seed, fertilizer, timely and proper plant protection measures, institutional credit, etc.

Gogoi (1989) in a study relating to the state of Assam

observed that frequent breakdowns of the wells, irregular supply of electricity in case of deep tube-wells, lack of proper time schedule for raising different crops in case of surface flow schemes are some of the factors hindering full utilisation of irrigation potential created. He also found that inadequate agricultural extension facilities and lack of coordination among various departments in the development of irrigation in the sample district were also responsible for under-utilisation of created irrigation potential.

The problem of underutilisation of irrigation water could be solved to some extent by improving the allocation distribution and supply of canal water and making it available in time to the cultivators. Patel and Patel (1983) found that inadequate supply of water was the main cause of low intensity of land use. In this context, the distribution system of water on rotation basis was considered as the best.

2.5.4 Relative Efficiency of Different Forms

Dhawan (1980) examined the comparative efficiencies of well irrigation system *versus* canal irrigation system in India. He found that land productivity measured in terms of foodgrain production per unit irrigated area in some selected regions in the country was significantly higher in case of well irrigation, being 5.2 to 6.0 tonnes per hectare than that of canal irrigation which was of the order of 2.1 to 2.9 tonnes per hectare. The study also pointed out that the increase in the productivity of net irrigated area was more pronounced in case of well irrigation than that of canal irrigation. This is borne by the fact that the productivity under well irrigation increased from 2.6 tonnes per hectare in late fifties to 6.0 tonnes per hectare in late seventies while the figure for the same in case of canal irrigation was 1.8 tonnes per hectare in the late fifties to 2.6 tonnes per hectare in late seventies.

The main objective of the study by Mellor and Moorti (1971) was to find out the relative profitability of different sources of minor irrigation works such as (i) state tube-wells, (ii) private tube-wells, and (iii) use of Persian wheels in Aligarh district of U.P. They observed that of the three models of irrigation, private tube-wells proved the most efficient. The farmers using water supplied by private tube-wells used water more intensively, and they grew two crops on proportionately a larger area of their holdings.

Puttaswamaiah's (1977) study tries to analyse the pros and cons of the economics of minor irrigation projects *vis-a-vis* the major irrigation projects in the light of empirical data available in the Indian context. According to him, the investments made in the irrigation sector should yield immediate returns and this is possible only when investments are made on small-scale irrigation schemes rather than on large scale ones. Nearly half of the irrigation potential can be utilised by taking up minor irrigation works alone. He opines that in the minor irrigation sector also, emphasis should be given on well irrigation as that is the only programme which will be within the reach of the small and marginal farmers.

In a study relating to the state of Maharashtra, Dhawan (1982) tried to measure the magnitude of increase in farm incomes due to public irrigation and to assess the extent to which these income increases bear positive association with farm size. The author concluded that the large farmers, on account of easy access to all inputs, had gained greater advantage of income as compared to small farmers.

2.5.5 Minor Irrigation Schemes

Venkataramani's (1974) study is related to the productivity of the minor irrigation programmes in Tamil Nadu. The author found a positive correlation between minor irrigation and productivity. It points to the possibility of increasing the productivity of land by harnessing in an optimum manner minor sources of irrigation. The study also found that minor sources of irrigation had been inherently viable. The benefits accruing from minor sources have been more than the expenditure expended upon them. A constraint that has been identified is that minor irrigation cannot be treated as a separate entity but should be considered alongside major and medium irrigation projects. But the study has certain shortcomings too. It is based entirely on secondary data. Primary survey at least for certain districts should have been undertaken.

Groundwater irrigation forms a part of minor irrigation in India. According to Pant (1991), the backwardness of agriculture in the eastern part of India is the underutilisation of available groundwater. Only 17 per cent of the potential of groundwater in the region is exploited as against an average of 27 per cent for the country as a whole (as in 1986). The author observes that extensive use of available groundwater could help improve cropping intensity, promote diversification and increase productivity. Pant believes that the question of ground-water exploitation and balanced development involves a variety of issues. These include subsidies to poor farmers and their impact, legislative and regulative aspects of ground-water exploitation, power supply and subsidized power for agriculture, technological and organisational alternatives for groundwater lift and its management, and finally, ground water markets and their pervasiveness.

Dhawan (1995) observed that at the national level ground-water resource is still far from depletion or over-exploitation. Only 30 per cent of the available groundwater resource (of the order of 385 billion cubic metre) was exploited for irrigation purpose in 1992. He observes disparity in groundwater exploitation across states and across river basins. For example, against a cent per cent utilisation of groundwater in Punjab, only 5 per cent is being annually utilised for irrigation purpose in Assam. Again, in Chandigarh depletion is said to have already started.

Dhawan opined that volumetric approach of groundwater estimate is more suitable than the area approach which is subject to a number of limitations and as such can give rise to an exaggerated picture of groundwater development.

Vaidyanathan (1996) in a study on "Depletion of Groundwater : Some Issues" observed that the productivity per unit of water tapped is much higher in case of groundwater compared to surface water. This is because (a) groundwater involves much less waste by way of conveyance and application losses and (b) farmers have much greater flexibility to adjust timing and the quantum of water application to the crop needs. On the issue of depletion of groundwater, he opined that certain parameters should be taken into account for judging whether a particular region has crossed the limits of sustainable use of groundwater. These include the location and boundaries of aquifers, their respective average annual recharge and extraction rates, the proportion of wells which are going dry and out of use, and the total area irrigated. A progressive lowering of groundwater table by itself may not always indicate overexploitation in so far as farmers change their crop-pattern and irrigation practices to make better use of available water.

An important issue associated with groundwater irrigation is the development of groundwater market. Pant (1991) noticed the development of groundwater market in many states of Eastern India during his field visit. The water was generally sold by affluent farmers to less affluent ones. At times, however, very small scheduled caste farmers who obtained a subsidy of 75 per cent for installing pumps and tube- wells sold water to their more affluent neighbours who preferred to buy water than to install their own tube-wells. In all states of the eastern region water was sold at an hourly rate. Rates varied from state to state and situation to situation but it ranged between Rs. 8 and Rs. 25 per hour from a 5 H. P. pump.

Satyasai *et al.* (1997) in a study in Ananṭapur district of

Andhra Pradesh found that the small farmers in the area had, in general, limited access to groundwater compared to large farmers. The groundwater markets prevalent in the area helped improve the access of small farmers to water. However, there was a cost to improving the equity as water was purchased at the rate or Rs. 7.70 and Rs. 50 per hour under hourly and crop sharing modes of payment respectively. These rates were 14 and 91 times higher than the operation and maintenance cost running a well for an hour incurred by the seller (Rs. 0.55) in the same order.

Groundwater market, developed as a result of exploitation of sources of groundwater for irrigation, may be highly monopolistic at times. Fujita and Hossain (1995) in their case study in a north-west Bangladesh village found that groundwater market in the area seemed to be highly monopolistic.

According to Shah and Raju (1987), localised, fragmented, village based groundwater markets are far more pervasive and far more important in their size, role and implications than most researchers and policy-makers imagine.

Tube-well irrigation as a part of minor irrigation has expanded at a rapid rate since the mid-sixties in India.

The most common modes of extracting groundwater for irrigation are shallow and deep tube-wells depending on the surface level of groundwater. Appu (1974) noticed the functioning of a special type of tube-well in Saharsa district of Bihar where bamboo instead of steel was used as pipes for extracting water. Since the cost of this type of tube-well was very low, even the small and marginal farmers in the district also could reap benefit from groundwater irrigation.

Choudhury (1971) studied the economics of tube-well irrigation in Nadia District of West Bengal. The study found that the irrigated area under *rabi* crops was much higher than under *kharif* crops for all the tube wells except one in Krishnanagar-1. High cost involved in the installation of deep tube-wells and excessive fragmentation of land compelled the medium and large farmers to turn towards shallow tube-wells which can irrigate nearly 10 acres of land.

Dhawan (1982) pointed out that high degree of indivisibility in Indian farm conditions was responsible for the non-diffusion of tube-well technology during the first half of this century. In the wake of development planning that contributed towards easing numerous constraints of the Indian economy tube-well indivisibility witnessed substantial reduction, thereby inducing many farmers to invest in their own tube-wells. The author feels that direct participation of the government is important for exploiting the groundwater resources in the east Gangetic plains. Dhawan also identified two problems of groundwater management— (i) overexploitation leading to a permanent lowering of the water table and (ii) mutual discord among the users of water. A change over from dug-well to tube-well technology by farmers of low rainfall tracts accentuates this danger. Therefore, the state has to keep a close vigil on the water table in western parts of the Indo-Gangetic plains.

2.6 Conclusion

Thus, it is clear from above discussion that irrigation not only promotes growth in the productivity of agriculture but also contributes towards stabilization of agricultural production. However, for ensuring a better performance of irrigation schemes, management aspects have to be given due attention. The main system management is considered a key to better performance of irrigation projects. It involves planning, decision-making, and operation of controls and communication from manager's level to farmers' level. Due to lack of these, a number of projects have been suffering from the problem of underutilisation of irrigation water. Underutilisation of irrigation potential created, however, involves a lot more issues. Firstly, the definition of the term 'underutilisation' itself is to be clearly understood and the reference periods to which the figures of potential created and potential utilised relate are to be laid down unambiguously in terms of the sowing season. The determination of the area of irrigation potential should be done after taking into account the water requirements of the cropping pattern prescribed by the project authorities. Full utilisation of irrigation potential, although desirable, is very difficult to achieve. According to economists, about 90 per cent utilisation can be considered good enough. Under-utilisation is found to be most marked in case of surface flow irrigation schemes. Apart from inefficient management of water supplies at the system level, the other notable factors for low utilisation of irrigation potential are found to be the faulty design of outlets and canals, delay in the construction of feeder canals and channels carrying water from main canal to the field, non-availability of inputs like fertilizers, hybrid seeds, pesticides and new agricultural implements, absence of supporting land reform measures like consolidation of holding and land levelling, etc. Tail-end deprivation is another issue associated with the problem of under-utilisation. This takes place in surface flow irrigation schemes mainly because of resistance of the cultivators in upper reaches in releasing water for the farmers below the canal for one reason or the other. Lack of cooperation among the bureaucracy and the beneficiaries, and also between various departments involved in implementing irrigation programmes, erratic supply of electricity in case of lift irrigation schemes, etc. are some other factors contributing to the problem of underutilisation of irrigation potential. While all these problems cannot be solved at the farm level because of their technical nature, some of the problems in the field can be overcome by developing appropriate institutional framework ensuring better involvement of stakeholders in maintenance and management of the schemes. All these issues need careful attention before making further investment in an irrigation project since creating irrigation potential in a scheme, particularly in the major project, is a costly affair.

REFERENCES

Alagh, Y. K. (1987), *The Next Phase of Water Planning*, Inaugural Address at the First National Water Convention held in Delhi, November 12.

Ali, A. N. M. Irshad (1975), *A Study on the Impact of Mayong Lift Irrigation Project*, Agro-Economic Research Centre for North East, Jorhat.

Appu, P. S. (1974), "The Bamboo Tube-well : A Low Cost Device for Exploiting Ground Water", *Economic and Political Weekly*, Vol. 26, p. A-63.

Bhingraj, S. M. (1987), "Underutilisation of Irrigation Resources in India", *Commerce*, Vol. 154, No. 3959, April 4-10.

Burt, Charles M. (2007), "Volumetric Irrigation Water Pricing Considerations", *Irrigation and Drainage Systems*, 21.1, 133-144 (*http://works.bepress.com/cburt/56/*) accessed on 6.8.2009

Chambers, Robert (1992), *Managing Canal Irrigation — Practical Analysis for South Asia*, Oxford and IBH Publishing Company Private Limited, New Delhi.

Chatterjee, Nandini (1995), *Irrigated Agriculture*, Rawat Publishers, Jaipur and New Delhi.

Choudhury, B. K. (1971), *Economics of Tube-Well Irrigation in West Bengal*, Agro-Economic Research Centre, Viswabharati.

Clark, Colin (1970), *The Economics of Irrigation (2nd edition)*, ELBS and Pergamon Press, Oxford.

Cornish, G., *et al.* (2004), *Water Charging in Irrigated Agriculture : An Analysis of International Experience*, Food and Agriculture Organization of the United Nations (*http://www.fao.org/docrep/008/y5690e/y5690e07.htm*) accessed on 6.8.2009

Dhawan, B. D. (1980), "Underutilisation of Ground Water Resources : A Case Study of East U. P.", *Economic and Political Weekly*, No. 39.

Dhawan, B. D. (1982), *Development of Tube-Well Irrigation in India*, Agricole Publishing Academy, New Delhi.

Dhawan, B. D. (1986), "Irrigation and Water Management in India : Perception of Problems and their Resolution", *Indian Journal of Agricultural Economics*, Vol. 41, No. 3, July-September.

Dhawan, B. D. (1988), *Irrigation in India's Agricultural Development*, Sage Publications, New Delhi.

Dhawan, B. D. (1995), "Magnitude of Groundwater Exploitation", *Economic and Political Weekly*, April 8.

Dhawan, B. D. (1997), *India's Irrigation Sector : Myths and Realities*, Presidential Address of 57th Annual Conference of the Indian Society of Agricultural Economics held at G.B. Pant University of Agriculture and Technology, Pantnagar. (Mimeo).

Dhawan, B. D. and Dutta, H. S. (1992), "Impact of Irrigation on Multiple Cropping", *Economic and Political Weekly*, March 28.

Dutta, K. S. and Chang-Bao-Wen (1986), "Underutilisation of Canal Irrigation in Sona Command Area of Bihar", *Agricultural Situation in India*, Vol. XLI, No. 8.

Easter, K. W. (1974), "Improving Village Irrigation System : An Example for India", *Land Economics*, Vol. 53, No.1.

Fujita, K. and Hossain, F. (1995), "Role of the Groundwater Market in Agricultural Development and Income Distribution : A Case Study in North-West Bangladesh Village", *The Developing Economics*, XXXII-4.

Gadgil, D. R. (1948), *Economic Effects of Irrigation – Report of Survey of the Direct and Indirect Benefits of Godavari and Pravara Canals*, Gokhale Institute of Politics and Economics, Pune.

Gogoi, Bharati (1993), "Irrigation and Agricultural Development in Assam" in K. Alam (1993) (ed.) *Agricultural Development in North-East India : Constraints and Prospects*, Deep and Deep Publications, New Delhi.

Gogoi, K. (1989), "Irrigation in Assam" in P. C. Goswami (Ed.) (1989), *Agriculture in Assam*, Assam Institute of Development Studies, Guwahati.

Gohain, D. and Gogoi, K. (1986), *Problems of Underutilisation of Irrigation Potentials*, Agro Economic Research Centre for N.E. India, Jorhat (Mimeographed).

Government of India (1966), *Evaluation of Major Irrigation Projects : Some Case Studies*, Programme Evaluation Organisation, Planning Commission.

ICAR (1972), *Proceedings of the Symposium on Cropping Pattern in India*, Indian Council of Agricultural Research, p. 15.

Jha, U. M. (1984), *Irrigation and Agricultural Development*, Deep and Deep Publications, New Delhi.

Mellor, John W. and Moorti, T. V. (1971), "Dilemma of State Tube-Wells", *Economic and Political Weekly*, Vol. 3, No. 6, March 27.

Mitra, Ashok K. (1984), "Managing Irrigation System in Drought Prone Areas", *Indian Journal of Agricultural Economics*, Vol. 39, No. 3, July-September.

Mitra, Ashok K. (1987), *Planning and Management of Surface Irrigation in Drought Prone Areas,* Gokhale Institute of Politics and Economics, Pune.

Mitra, Ashok K. (1991), "Water Resource Management : Discussion at Agricultural Economics Conference", *Economic and Political Weekly,* Review of Agriculture, September. 28, p. A-115.

Narayanamoorthy, A. (1996), "Electric Pumpset and Groundwater Management— Macro and Micro Evidence of India", *Water Resources Journal,* June.

Palanisami, K. (1984), *Irrigation Water Management—the Determinants of Canal Water Distribution in India—A Micro Analysis,* Agricole Publishing Academy, New Delhi.

Pant, Niranjan (1981), *Some Aspects of Irrigation Administration: A Case Study of Kosi Project (Bihar),* Naya Prakash, Calcutta.

Pant, Niranjan (1991), "Groundwater Issues in Eastern India" in Ruth Meinzen-Dick and Mark Svendsen (ed.) (1991), *Future Directions for Indian Irrigation — Research and Policy Issues,* International Food Policy Research Institute, Washington D.C.

Patel, S. A. and Patel, H. F. (1983), "Irrigation Practices and Efficiency of Water Use—A study of Machchu 1 Irrigation Project Area in Gujarat," *Agricultural Situation in India,* p.12, October.

Pawar, Chandrakanth T. (1989), *Impact of Irrigation : A Regional Perspective,* Himalaya Publishing House, Bombay.

Phukan, Umananda (1985), *A Study on the Impact of Deep Tube-well Irrigation on Crop Production in Jorhat District of Assam,* Agro Economic Research Centre for North-East India, Assam Agricultural University, Jorhat.

Phukan, Umananda (1986), *A Study on the Impact of Deep Tube-well Irrigation on Crop Production in Kamrup District of Assam,* Agro Economic Research Centre for North-East India, Assam Agricultural University, Jorhat.

Puttaswamaiah, K. (1977), *Irrigation Projects in India—Towards a New Policy,* Nrusimha Publications, Bangalore.

Rao, C. H. H., Ray, S. K. and Subbarao, K. (1988), *Unstable Agriculture and Drought,* Vikas, New Delhi.

Reddy, P. Sanjeeva (1997), *Different Sources of Irrigation,* Manak Publications Private Limited, New Delhi.

Satpathy, T. (1984), *Irrigation and Economic Development,* Asish Publishing House, New Delhi.

Satya Sai, K. J. S. (1990), "Impact of Irrigation on Intensity of Land Utilisation" in Tyagi, N. K., Joshi, P. K. and Singh, N. T. (ed.) *National Symposium on Management of Irrigation System*, Central Soil Salinity Research Institute, Karnal.

Satyasai, K. J. S., Kumar Praduman and Mruthyunjaya (1997), "Terms of Transactions in Groundwater Markets : A Study in Anantapur District of Andhra Pradesh", *Indian Journal of Agricultural Economics*, Vol. 52, No. 4, October-December.

Sawant, S. D. (1986), "Irrigation and Water use" in Indian Society of Agricultural Economics (1986) *Indian Agricultural Development since Independence*, Oxford & IBH.

Shah, Tushaar and K. Vengama Raju (1987), "Working of Ground-water Market in Andhra Pradesh and Gujarat : Results of two Village Studies", *Economic and Political Weekly*, Vol. 22, No. 13, March 26.

Singh, Baldev (1991), "Impact of Irrigation on Income, Employment and Land Use Pattern in Punjab", *Indian Journal of Agricultural Economics*, Vol. XLVI, No. 4.

Srinivasmurthy, A.P. (1990), *Irrigation Planning in India*, Himalaya Publishing House, Bombay.

Stern, P. H. (1979), *Small Scale Irrigation*, Intermediate Technology Publications, London, U.K.

Sukla, L. and Gurjar, R. K. (1990), *Canal Irrigation Management*, Agricole Publishing Academy, New Delhi.

Swaminathan, M. S. (1981), *Irrigation and Our Agricultural Future*, First Ajudhia Nath Khosla Lecture, delivered at the University of Roorkee, Reproduced by Centre for Monitoring Indian Economy, Mumbai.

Vaidyanathan, A. (1996), "Depletion of Ground-water Exploitation : Some Issues", *Indian Journal of Agricultural Economics*, Vol. 51, No.1 and 2, January-June.

Venkataramani, G. (1974), *Minor Irrigation in Tamil Nadu*, Sangam Publishers, Madras for Madras Institute of Development Studies (MIDS).

Wade, Robert (1978), "Water Supply as an Instrument of Agricultural Policy — A Case Study", *Economic and Political Weekly*, March 25.

Yousuf, Mohammed (1990), *Irrigation : Plan, Practice, Perspective*, Ajanta Publications, Delhi.

3

Irrigation in the Agricultural Economy of Assam

3.1 The Agricultural Economy of Assam

3.1.1 Location, Physical Features and Climatic Condition of the State

Assam forms the core of the North-Eastern states. With a geographical area of 78,438 sq. kilometres it is located between the latitudes of '24°08′ N and 27°09′ N and the longitudes of 89°42′ E and 96°10′ E. The location of the state is strategically very important. She shares her boundary with a number of Indian states and a couple of foreign countries. To the north of the state are the kingdom of Bhutan and the state of Arunachal Pradesh. Nagaland, Manipur and Arunachal Pradesh are to the east of the state, Mizoram to her south, Tripura, Meghalaya and the Republic of Bangladesh to her south-west and finally, the state of West Bengal to her west.

The state is comprised of three broad natural divisions, the largest being the Brahmaputra Valley — a long strip of plain land extending from west to north-east in the northern part of the state. The valley derives its name from the mighty river Brahmaputra which runs from north-east to west through a distance of 450 kilometres, splitting the valley into two long strips. The valley comprises about 72 per cent of the total geographical area of the state. In the southern part of the state is another river valley, namely the Barak Valley with the river Barak passing through it. The region is relatively small accounting for only about 9 per cent of the total area of the state. In between the valleys lies the hilly region comprising the districts of Karbi Anglong and North Cachar Hills. This region constitutes about 19 per cent of the total area of the state and is relatively sparse in population.

The climate of Assam is characterised by generally very wet summer months followed by sunny winters. The south-west monsoon normally operates for a longer spell in Assam compared to the rest of the country. The monsoon rain normally starts from early June and continues till October. Even pre-monsoon heavy showers in late April and May are not uncommon. During the summer months temperature generally varies between 25° and 40° celsius. The winter months from November to February are mostly dry. The temperature in the winter sometimes falls below 5° celsius in some places. Humidity remains high (70%) with minor recess during the months of March and April.

The intensity of rainfall in the state is very heavy during the monsoon season comprising the months from June to September. The average rainfall during this period is about 1407 millimetre. The two months of January and February in winter season witness, on an average, rainfall of about 42.9 millimetre. As a whole, the state enjoys an average rainfall of about 2218 millimetre, sometimes exceeding the figure and sometimes falling short of that. For the year 2006 (January 2006 to December 2006), the state enjoyed, on an average, a rainfall of about 1741.0 millimetre (Government of Assam, 2007). Table 3.1 shows the rainfall in the state for the year 2006.

Table 3.1 : Seasonwise Rainfall in Assam (from January. 2006 to December. 2006)

(Rainfall in millimetre)

Winter Season Jan. to Feb.		*Summer March to May*		*Monsoon June to Sept.*		*Post-Monsoon Oct. to Dec.*		*Total Jan. to Dec.*	
Normal	Actual	Normal	Actual	Normal	Actual	Normal	Actual	Normal	Actual
42.9	40.6	590.2	430.5	1407.3	1261.5	177.4	90.7	2217.8	1741.0

Source : Statistical Hand Book of Assam 2007, Government of Assam.

3.1.2 Demography

According to 2001 census, the provisional total population for the state is 26,638,407 out of which 13,787,799 are male and 12,850,608 are females. The population of the state in 1991 was 22,414,322. Thus it has recorded a decadal variation of about 18.85 per cent. Assam has witnessed a very high rate of growth in population during the post-independence period. During the two decades of 1951-61 and 1961-71 the state recorded decennial rate of growth in population of 34.97 per cent and 34.95 per cent respectively. The corresponding growth rates for the country as a whole were 21.64 per cent and 24.80 per cent respectively. The growth rate of population of the state for the two decades 1971-81 and 1981-91 was 23.4 per cent and 23.8 per cent respectively whereas the corresponding figure for the country as a whole stood at 24.7 per cent and 23.8 per cent respectively (Government of Assam, 2002). The relatively high rate of growth in population as compared to the country as a whole is indicative of the substantial contribution of net immigration to the population of Assam during this period. The density of the state has also remained very high for quite a few decades. According to the provisional population figures of 2001 census, the density of the state is 340 persons per square km as compared to 312 sq. km for the whole of India. In 1991, the density for India was found to be 273 per sq. km while that for Assam was at a higher level at 286 per sq. km.

3.1.3 The Economy and the Place of Agriculture in It

Per capita income is considered to be the indicator of the

growth of an economy. Assam stands somewhere near the bottom of the list of Indian states by per capita income. In 2007-08, the per capita income of Assam at constant prices (in 1999-2000 prices) was Rs. 15,526 which was about 36 per cent less than the per capita income of Rs.24, 295 for the country as a whole.. It is also noticed that the state has continued to lag behind the per capita income at national level. In fact, in the recent years, the gap of per capita income of Assam and India has widened further.

Although the share of tertiary sector in the State Domestic Product (SDP) of the state has gone up in recent years, the significance of agriculture and allied sector (comprised of agriculture, forestry and logging, fishery and mining and quarrying). has not reduced much. In 2007-08 the share of the primary sector in the State Domestic Product was 29.52 per cent while the corresponding figure for the country as a whole was 20.61 per cent. The share of secondary sector comprising manufacturing, construction, electricity, gas and water supply was relatively less. In 2007-08, this sector contributed about 14.93 per cent of the net State Domestic Product (SDP) while share of the tertiary sector was higher at 55.54 per cent. Thus the economy of the state has witnessed a lopsided deve-lopment in terms of a higher relative contribution of tertiary sector in the state domestic product. Agriculture and allied sector still is an important sector in the state's economy. Apart from contributing handsomely to the SDP, it is engaging directly about 69 per cent of the total workforce of the state.

3.1.4 The Land Use Pattern

As per the data available from the Directorate of Economics and Statistics, Government of Assam, the total geographical area of the state is 78,438 sq. km. At present, only about one-third of this area is being put under cultivation. In the year 2003-04 (the latest year for which figures on total area and classification of area are at present available), the net sown area was 27,52,601 hectares which is approximately 35.09 per cent of the total geographical area of the state. The total crop area for the year was 39,56,842 hectares. The cropping intensity in the state thus works out to be 144 per cent. The land use pattern of the state for the year 2003-04 is given in Table 3.2.

Table 3.2 : Land Use Pattern of Assam in 2003-04

Total Geographical Area (in hectares)	*Not Available for Cultivation (in hectares)*	*Net Area Sown (in hectares)*	*Total Cropped Area (in hectares)*	*Area Sown More than Once (in hectares)*	*Cropping Intensity (in percentage)*
78,43,800	25,33,033	27,52,601	39,56,842	12,04,241	144

Source: Statistical Hand Book of Assam 2007, Directorate of Economics and Statistics, Government of Assam.

3.1.5 Pattern of Land Holding

In 2000-01, there were as many as 27,12,137 operational holdings in Assam, the average size of holdings being 1.15 hectares. About 63 per cent of these holdings were of size below one hectare and they together constituted only 21.29 per cent of the total area under all holdings. The distribution of operational holdings by size class for the reference year 2000-01 is shown in Table 3.3.

Table 3.3 : Operational Holdings by Size and Area Classification in Assam, 2000-01

Size Class of Holdings	*Number of Holdings*	*Percentage of Total Number of Holdings*	*Area under each Size Class (in hectares)*	*Percentage of Total Area under each Size Class*
(1)	*(2)*	*(3)*	*(4)*	*(5)*
Below 1 hectare	16,69,107	62.23	6,62,780	21.29
1 to 2 hectare	5,61,039	20.92	7,30,513	23.46
2 to 4 hectare	3,51,521	13.10	9,57,959	30.77
4 to 10 hectare	95,500	3.56	4,98,797	16.02
Above 10 hectare	4,970	0.19	2,63,529	8.46
All size total	26,82,137	100.00	31,13,578	100.00

Source : Statistical Hand Book of Assam, 2007, Directorate of Economics and Statistics, Government of Assam.

It is clear from the table that the distribution of operational holdings in the region is highly skewed with the concentration of more than half of the holdings in the lowest size class of below one hectare. In terms of area the holdings in the size class of below one hectare comprised about 21 per cent of total area under all holdings while the size class of two to four hectares accounts for the largest share of area of about 31 per cent.

3.1.6 Cropping Pattern

The cropping pattern in an economy is shown by the shares of different crops in the gross cropped area. It may undergo changes over time in response to changes in a number of factors, namely economic, technological and other environmental factors. The available latest figures on area under different crops in the state relate to the year 1998-99. The total area under crops in the state has been worked out by adding up the area under different field crops reported by the Directorate of Agriculture. Thus the total area under study excludes area under plantation and tree crops like tea, vegetables, banana, papaya, arecanut, etc. The exclusion of these crops may be justified on the ground that they stand on a different footing from the usual field crops like rice, wheat, jute, potato, etc. (Roy and Bezbaruah, 2002). The cropping pattern in Assam is dominated by rice. Out of a total gross cropped area of 39,40,649 hectares, 24,54,000 hectares (that is about 62.27%) were under rice in 1998-99. The share of rice in total cereals stood at 95.34 per cent which means that the share of other cereals comprising wheat, maize, other cereals and millets among themselves commanded only 4.66 per cent. Among rest of the crops cultivated in Assam, rape and mustard are the most important. In 1998-99, 7.33 per cent of total cropped area of the state was under these crops. Jute had a share of 2.00 per cent while the shares of sugarcane and potato were 0.76 per cent and 1.95 per cent of total cropped area respectively. Seasonwise, the rice crop in Assam is divided into three categories, viz. (a) Autumn rice, (b) Winter rice, and (c) Summer rice, each category deriving its name from the season in which the crop is harvested (Bezbaruah, 1994). Areawise, winter rice is the most important crop cultivated in the state. In 1998-99, the crop was cultivated in an area of 16,35,000 hectares which is about 66.63 per cent of the total area under rice in the state. The area under autumn and summer paddy taken together is much smaller compared to the area under winter paddy. In 1998-99, the total area under these two crops was 8,19,000 hectares which is about 33.37 per cent of the total area under rice in the state (Government of Assam, 2002). However, there has been a gradual decline in the area coverage under autumn paddy whereas the area under summer paddy is found to have increased. This is mainly because of the fact that the farmers have switched over the area under autumn paddy to summer paddy because of its high productivity. During 1998-99, the area coverage under autumn paddy was found to be 5.95 lakh hectares as compared to 6.07 hectares in 1997-98.

3.1.7 Present State of Agriculture

It is clear from the foregoing analysis that agriculture, although is the mainstay of the state's economy, is yet to experience the diversification essential for overall development of the state's economy. Rice is still the dominant crop grown. But the pattern of growth and productivity of the principal crop are not very high compared to the corresponding all-India figures. The backwardness of the state's agriculture is amply reflected in the low productivity of rice. In 1999-2000, the yield rate of rice in the state was 14.80 quintal per hectare against 33.50 quintal per hectare in Punjab, 32.80 quintal per hectare in Tamil Nadu, 29.70 quintal per hectare in Haryana, 26.90 quintal per hectare in Andhra Pradesh and 22.60 quintal per hectare in West Bengal. The all-India figure for the same was 19.90 quintal per hectare (CMIE, 2001). Thus the yield of the principal crop in the state is much lower than the national average, not to speak of agriculturally advanced states like Punjab, Haryana, Tamil Nadu, etc. It establishes that in the post-green revolution period, Assam has not been able to achieve agricultural prosperity at the same rate as most of the other traditionally agricultural regions in the country have. Fertilizer consumption is another indicator of the performance of agricultural sector in an economy. In Assam, the rate of fertilizer consumption is one of the lowest in the country. In 2002-03, the per hectare fertilizer consumption in the state was only 44.12 kg against 91.45 kg for the country as a whole. The rate, however, has shown significant increase over the years. While the rate was a meagre of 13.99 kg/hectare, it increased to 26.90 kg/hectare are in 1999-2000 and then to 44.12 kg/hectare are in 2002-03. Statewise fertilizer consumption per hectare in India during 1997-98 to 2003-04 is shown in Table 3.4.

Irrigation is considered as a prime factor for enhancing agricultural productivity. In fact, green revolution in the country took place for the first time in India in the alluvial plains of the North-West where assured and continuous supply of irrigation water was made available to the farmers. The agriculturally advanced states of the country are also rich in irrigation facility. But irrigation infrastructure in Assam is not very good. In 2003-04, only 6.20 per cent of the net sown area in the state was irrigated as against 96.31 per cent in Punjab, 84.01 per cent in Haryana and 73.70 per cent in Uttar Pradesh. The corresponding figure for the country as a whole was 39.11 per cent. Thus Assam has lagged behind even the national average in so far as proportion of net irrigated area to net sown area is concerned, not to speak of the agriculturally advanced states in the country. The gross irrigated area of the state under government sector in 2003-04 was 1,72,000 hectares of which as high as 88 per cent was irrigated by canals (CMIE, 2007).

Table 3.4 : Fertilizer Consumption in Different States

(kg/hectare)

States	*1997-98*	*1998-99*	*1999-2000*	*2000-01*	*2001-02*	*2002-03*	*2003-04*
(1)	*(2)*	*(3)*	*(4)*	*(5)*	*(6)*	*(7)*	*(8)*
Andhra Pradesh	139.64	147.37	162.68	160.54	153.42	144.71	149.84
Arunachal Pradesh	2.12	2.40	2.06	2.28	2.90	2.94	2.78
Assam	17.84	18.93	26.90	34.59	38.38	44.12	47.66
Bihar	108.29	102.65	–		96.03	95.79	88.19
Delhi	519.65	257.50	321.15	96.98	69.04	59.25	35.91
Goa	37.40	39.94	42.57	34.21	34.88	33.72	36.09
Gujarat	92.13	91.50	95.12	70.22	85.26	80.07	89.85
Haryana	136.49	132.66	149.58	152.13	155.74	153.21	159.97
H.P.	35.35	39.75	39.02	37.50	42.00	41.77	49.22
Jammu & Kashmir	56.35	65.53	58.18	58.28	63.09	60.13	72.23
Karnataka	94.85	93.31	105.14	109.76	107.06	95.37	80.33
Kerala	73.92	62.32	70.41	57.32	59.19	67.58	65.03
M.P.	60.39	48.15	46.21	39.07	40.34	38.97	49.70
Maharastra	73.84	74.99	86.37	75.18	75.40	73.68	64.83
Manipur	63.71	79.06	93.83	105.45	104.89	122.80	125.70
Meghalaya	13.17	17.37	14.91	13.66	18.87	19.86	17.35
Mizoram	9.00	8.79	24.84	13.51	20.53	20.70	15.00
Nagaland	2.23	3.43	2.78	1.38	6.78	1.49	1.84
Orissa	33.64	35.51	42.24	40.52	39.17	37.00	37.77
Punjab	167.81	177.71	175.43	166.69	169.97	184.25	195.20
Rajasthan	35.27	33.98	42.37	34.57	37.93	41.61	35.94
Sikkim	5.93	8.82	7.26	8.57	9.53	9.84	3.64
Tamil Nadu	143.72	143.48	161.36	151.94	150.65	143.16	134.14
Tripura	21.48	22.13	18.57	21.50	40.01	26.75	37.73
Uttar Pradesh	122.17	121.03	125.18	–	131.73	128.62	127.78
West Bengal	105.72	103.56	129.05	119.02	120.48	122.77	115.54
India	84.98	87.08	95.23	88.93	91.13	91.45	88.11

Source : Agriculture, Centre for Monitoring Indian Economy, March 2006, Mumbai.

Thus the present state of agriculture in Assam is not very satisfactory. The new agricultural technology of HYV—chemical fertilizer considered to be the main instrument of green revolution in the country—has failed to diffuse in the state. One of the main constraints on diffusion of new agricultural technology in the state has been identified as the underdevelopment of irrigation (Bezbaruah, 1994; Goswami, 1992). The entire state, except for a small area on its central part comprised parts of Nagaon and Karbi Anglong districts, receives abundant rainfall. But the rainfall is mostly concentrated in the monsoon season from June to September and the weather is mainly dry in the rest of the year. This makes irrigation important if the farmers have to take up the practice of multiple cropping.

3.2 Water Resources and Ultimate Irrigation Potential

The state can boast of a huge amount of surface as well as groundwater resources. The Brahmaputra and the Barak and their tributaries are the two major sources of surface water in the state. The Brahmaputra is ranked fourth among the large rivers of the world in terms of discharge at the mouth at 19,830 cubic metre per second (Goswami, 1989). According to an estimate, the average annual water flow of the country is 1853 cubic kilometre out of which the Brahmaputra and the Barak alone account for 628 cubic kilometre (i.e. 33.9% of the average annual flow of the country). The water resource potential of the river basins in India is estimated to be around 186.96 million hectometre and that of ground water to be 45.22 million hectometre. Significantly, the two river basins of the state (i.e. the Brahmaputra and the Barak) account for as high as 32 per cent of the country's total surface water potential. This clearly shows the enormous amount of surface water available in the state. However, these huge amount of water resources in the state are yet to be fully exploited. While much water continues to annually flow down the Brahmaputra and its tributaries in the state, most of it goes unutilised. So is the case with the Barak and its tributaries in the valley in the southern part of the state.

Besides the water flowing in the rivers, Assam is richly endowed with groundwater reserves. According to the Central Ground Water Board, the gross groundwater reserve for the state as a whole stands at 24,719 million cubic metre. Even after leaving aside about 15 per cent of this amount for domestic and industrial use, an amount of 21,011 million cubic metre is available for irrigation. But as in 1997, only 5

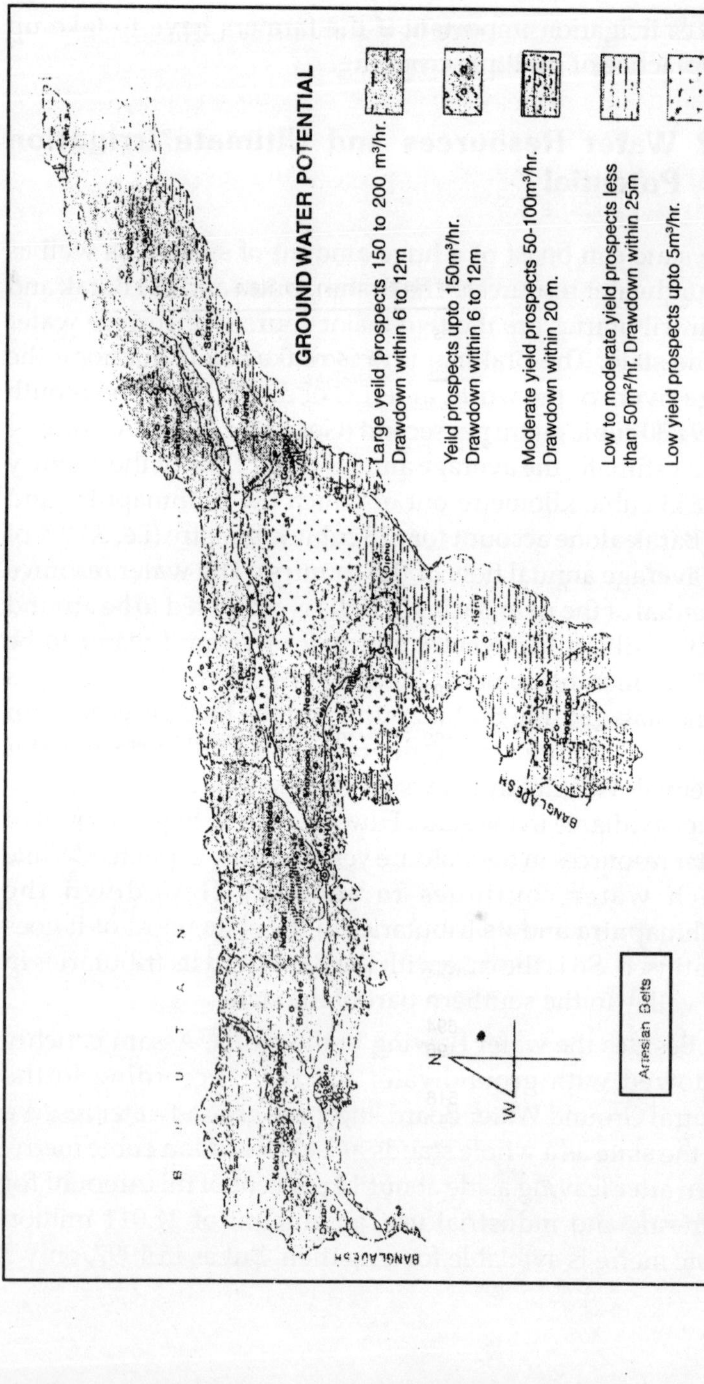

Fig. 3.1 : Ground Water Potential in Assam

per cent of this amount were being annually utilised. The unutilised 95 per cent of the groundwater can be used to irrigate an additional area of 14,86,461 hectares of land which is about 38 per cent of the gross cropped area of the state. The districtwise distribution of groundwater reserve in the state is given in Table 3.5.

Table 3.5 : Ground Water Resources in the State

Sl. No.	*District*	*Groundwater Resources (Million cubic metre)*			*Net Annual Ground-water Draft (Million m³)*	*Balance Ground-water Resource (Million m³)*	*Potential for more Irrigation (Area in hectares)*
		Gross	*Reserved for Domestic/ Industrial use*	*Available for Irrigation*			
(1)	*(2)*	*(3)*	*(4)*	*(5)*	*(6)*	*(7)*	*(8)*
1	Bongaigaon	592					
2	Goalpara	494	163	923	45	878	63,538
3	Dhubri	1,300	195	1,105	64	1,041	80,077
4	Kokrajhar	1,580	237	1,343	35	1,308	1,00,615
5	Barpeta	1,161	174	987	56.07	931	71,615
6	Nalbari	639					
7	Kamrup	1,229	280	1,588	108	1,480	1,13,846
8	Darrang	1,407	211	1,196	73	1,123	86,385
9	Sonitpur	1,615	242	1,373	110	1,262	97,077
10	Morigaon	321					
11	Nagaon	935	188	1,068	169	899	69,154
12	Golaghat	1,794	488	2,767	77	2,690	2,06,923
13	Jorhat	1,461					
14	Sibsagar	1,658	249	1,409	35	1,374	1,05,692
15	Dibrugarh	1,635	520	2,947	87	2,860	2,20,000
16	Tinsukia	1,832					
17	Lakhimpur	1,167	424	2,403	75	2,328	1,79,078
18	Dhemaji	1,660					
19	Cachar	817	123	694	1	693	53,307
20	Hailakandi	98	35	196	7	190	14,615
21	Karimganj	133					
22	N.C. Hills	607	91	516	0	515	39,615
23	Karbi Anglong	585	88	497	0	497	38,231
	Total	24,719	3,708	21,011	942	20,069	14,86,461

Source: Central Ground Water Board, Government of India, Guwahati.

Moreover, this groundwater is also easily extractable in most parts of the Brahmaputra Valley. As Das (1984) puts it, "The entire Brahmaputra Valley can be considered as a vast reservoir of groundwater. The water table is generally within 5 metres below the land surface except in a narrow belt of 10 to 15 kilometres of width in the northern side running along the foothills of the Himalayas known as the 'Bhabar' belt. In this belt water table generally lies at a depth of 15 to 35 metres below the land surface. Development of groundwater through shallow and deep tube-wells is feasible in the entire Brahmaputra Valley."

In the Brahmaputra valley again, there are certain pockets where both shallow and deep tube-wells result in spontaneously flowing wells. These pockets are known as 'artesian belts'. Erstwhile districts of Kamrup, Nagaon and Sibsagar include the three distinct artesian belts in the Brahmaputra valley. Because of the depth and pressure of the water level, extracting water through wells requires no additional power thereby making well irrigation extremely cost-effective in these areas.

However, the prospect of groundwater irrigation in the hilly region (i.e. the Central Assam Range) is generally limited to the small inter-mountain valleys. In the Barak Valley region too, groundwater layer and reserve are generally unsuitable for setting up groundwater based irrigation systems.

The ultimate irrigation potential in the state has been estimated at 27 lakh hectares compared to 1135 lakh hectares for the country as a whole (Government of India, 1994-95). Out of the targetted total of 27 lakh hectares of land to be irrigated, 10 lakh hectares are to be covered by major and medium irrigation projects and the rest 17 lakh hectares are to be brought under minor irrigation schemes. Again, of the land area proposed to be covered under minor irrigation schemes, 7 lakh hectares of land area is proposed to be irrigated by surface source whereas the rest 10 lakh hectares are to be covered by groundwater source. The Central Ground Water Board in consultation with the State Irrigation Department has assessed the irrigation potential from groundwater source as under :

(i) Dug-well = 1,41,000 nos. @ 0.5 hectares each = 0.705 lakh hectares.
(ii) Shallow Tube Well (STW) = 2,41,724 nos. @ 3 hectares each = 7.252 lakh hectares.
(iii) Deep Tube Well (DTW) = 5,000 nos. @ 40 hectares each = 2.000 lakh hectares.
Total = 9.957 lakh hectares @ 10.00 lakh hectares

3.3 Development of Irrigation Infrastructure in Assam

3.3.1 Prior to Independence

Before independence, the irrigation schemes undertaken in India were mainly of protective type; these programmes were taken up only in those areas where famine was a periodic phenomenon. Assam was excluded from these programmes because of the misconstrued notion that this state falls under a high rainfall zone and as such the need for irrigation was not felt. Irrigation, however, had been practised in the state from very early times especially by the plains tribal peasants in the foothill regions, by digging small canals (locally called *'dongs'*) from the streams flowing down the hill slope (Das, 1984). Later on, when the Department of Flood Control and Irrigation was created, it found the *'dongs'* handy, as a first measure, to replace the temporary works by constructing permanent structures to provide for a stabilised system of minor irrigation to the cultivators. As a result, 32 minor irrigation schemes completed by the Flood Control and Irrigation Department during the first three plans were confined to those districts where the use of *'dongs'* in agricultural field was more prominent.

A number of departments, viz. Agriculture, Flood Control and Irrigation etc. were involved in development of irrigation in the state during the early years. The minor irrigation schemes costing Rs. 4 lakhs or below were previously implemented by the Engineering wing of the State Agriculture Department. Those costing between Rs. 4 lakhs and Rs. 15 lakhs were implemented by the Flood Control and Irrigation Department. The schemes costing Rs. 15 lakh to Rs. 5 crore, according to the old classification, were termed as medium irrigation schemes, and those above Rs. 5 crore were major schemes. All the medium irrigation schemes were then implemented by the Flood Control and Irrigation Department, Government of Assam. It was only after 1974, the year when the department of Irrigation was created that all the Government irrigation schemes—minor, major and medium—were being implemented by the irrigation department.

Government sponsored irrigation schemes were taken up in the state only from the year of independence (1947). The power pump irrigation scheme was initiated in the state in 1947-48 with the object of extending the cultivation of spring paddy during the dry winter season in the flood affected areas as an insurance against the ravage on summer and winter paddy crops by floods. Thus, as Das remarked "In such areas efforts were concentrated more on protection of agricultural fields from floods rather than providing irrigation for growing crops during flood free periods."

Prior to the First Five-Year Plan, irrigation in the state was not developed in an organised way. During the period, only 2 minor irrigation schemes were completed bringing under their command a total gross area of 5100 acres and a net area of 3200 acres. An important minor irrigation scheme in the pre-plan period was Jingia Irrigation scheme in the present Sonitpur district (Sharma,1992).

3.3.2 During the Plan Periods

Up to the Third Plan the programmes of development of irrigation in the state were based mainly on minor irrigation schemes. No major or medium irrigation scheme was constructed up to this period. At the end of the Third Five-Year Plan, a total of 46.627 thousand hectares of land was brought under the coverage of irrigation facility and this was done with the help of minor irrigation schemes only.

It was only during the Third Five-Year Plan (1961-66) that two medium projects, namely the Jamuna Irrigation Project (Nagaon and Karbi Anglong) and the Sukla Irrigation Project (Kamrup) were started for the first time. The projects have already been completed and are presently in operation. Between 1970 and 1976 a number of irrigation projects were taken up for execution. These include Longa Irrigation Scheme (1972-73), Dikhari (1975-76) and Dekadong (1975-76) in medium category and Dhansiri (1975-76), Bordikarai (1974-75) and Integrated Kollong (1975-76) in the category of major irrigation schemes. Some of these schemes are already completed and some are in different stages of construction.

The Jamuna Irrigation Scheme is the first medium flow irrigation project in Assam, located primarily in the southern part of Nagaon district. This includes a small part of Karbi Anglong district too. The project was started in the year 1964-65 at an original estimate of Rs. 192.3 lakh and was completed in the year 1968-69. The original estimate was subsequently revised to Rs. 396.0 lakh in 1969. But the expenditure as against the revised estimate is reported to be Rs. 434.3 lakh.

The Sukla Irrigation Project which is another flow scheme is situated in the districts of Kamrup and Nalbari. The project was taken up in the year 1964-65 at an estimated cost of Rs.2.98 crore and was proposed to be completed by the year 1972. However, it could be completed only in 1978-79 at a total cost of Rs. 4.90 crores. According to the Second Revised Project Report by Sukla Irrigation Division, 1977, the gross command area of the project is 22,612.7 hectares while the net irrigated area proposed is 17,184.9 hectares.

It is worth mentioning that Jamuna and Sukla Irrigation schemes were started initially as medium irrigation schemes as per classification based on financial criteria. But later on, when classification of irrigation schemes started to be based on culturable command area (CCA), they were re-classified as major irrigation schemes. Till date, Jamuna and Sukla are the only two completed major schemes in the state. Apart from them, Dhansiri, Integrated Kollong, Bordikarai and Champamati are the other major irrigation projects undertaken by Irrigation Department, but these are yet to be completed. It is interesting to note that some of these major irrigation schemes were taken up for execution long time back (1970s). The undue delay in completion of the schemes has resulted in escalation of the cost of the projects.

3.3.2 (a) Major and Medium Irrigation Schemes Currently in Operation

At present there are 10 (ten) completed major and medium irrigation projects in the state. These include Longa FIP, Bhumki FIP, Rupahi FIP, Dekadong FIP, Koliabor FIP, improvement of Kulsik FIP, Harguti FIP and Dikhari FIP under medium category apart from the major schemes as already stated. Construction of another nine projects including four major projects is at present going on. Particulars of major and medium irrigation projects in the state are presented in Table 3.6.

Table 3.6 : Particulars of Major and Medium Irrigation Projects in Assam

Sl. No.	*Name of Irrigation Project*	*District*	*Classi-fication*	*Present Status*	*Type*	*Estimated Potential (in hectares)*
(1)	*(2)*	*(3)*	*(4)*	*(5)*	*(6)*	*(7)*
1.	Sukla	Kamrup/ Nalbari	Major	Completed	Flow	15.635
2	Jamuna	Nagaon	Major	Completed	Flow	30,996
3	Dhansiri	Darrang	Major	Ongoing	Flow	68,976
4	Champamati	Kokrajhar	Major	Ongoing	Flow	24,994
5	Integrated Kollong	Nagaon	Major	Ongoing	Lift	34,000
6	Bordikarai	Sonitpur	Major	Ongoing	Flow	25,532
7	Longa	Kokrajhar	Medium	Completed	Flow	4,960
8.	Horguti	Karbi Anglong	Medium	Completed	Flow	2,800
9.	Dikhari	Karbi Anglong	Medium	Completed	Flow	2,861
10	Kaliabor	Nagaon	Medium	Completed	Lift	13,560
11	Improvement of Kulsik	Darrang	Medium	Completed	Flow	3,000
12	Bhumki	Barpeta	Medium	Completed	Flow	4,200
13	Dekadong	Barpeta	Medium	Completed	Flow	6,050
14	Kaldiya	Barpeta	Medium	Ongoing	Flow	16,500
15	Pahumara	Barpeta	Medium	Ongoing	Flow	12,955
16	Borolia	Nalbari & Kamrup	Medium	Ongoing	Flow	13,562
17	Buridihing	Dibrugarh	Medium	Ongoing	Lift	5,054
18	Hawaipur	Karbi Anglong	Medium	Ongoing	Lift	3,840
19	Rupahi	Barpeta	Medium	Completed	Flow	3,992

Source : Statistical Cell, Irrigation Department, Government of Assam.

3.3.2 (b) Development of Minor Irrigation Schemes in the Public Sector

State Irrigation Department is also in the charge of setting up of minor irrigation schemes under government sector. Up to 31-3-2001, the Department sets up a total of 1568 numbers of minor irrigation schemes. These include different forms of minor schemes, namely surface flow, surface lift and groundwater lift including deep tube wells (DTW). In addition, a total of 1584 numbers of minor schemes are in various stages of construction. Table 3.7 shows the districtwise break up of minor irrigation schemes completed in the state up to 31-3-2001 and districtwise number of schemes ongoing as on 1-4-2001 respectively.

Table 3.7 : Districtwise Number of Minor Irrigation Schemes Completed up to 31-3- 2001 and Ongoing as on 1-4-2001 (including CAD/WC Schemes)

Sl. No.	*District*	*No. of Schemes Installed up to 31-3-2001*	*No. of Ongoing Schemes as on 1-4-2001*
(1)	*(2)*	*(3)*	*(4)*
1	Kokrajhar	98	40
2	Goalpara	37	96
3	Bongaigaon	31	39
4	Dhubri	84	93
5	Barpeta	60	70
6	Nalbari	70	48
7	Kamrup	199	158
8	Nagaon	222	248
9	Morigaon	83	43
10	Darrang	63	72
11	Sonitpur	83	53
12	Lakhimpur	43	52
13	Dhemaji	32	27
14	Jorhat	77	50
15	Golaghat	63	45
16	Sibsagar	75	59
17	Dibrugarh	28	37
18	Tinsukia	34	28
19	Cachar	21	53
20	Hailakandi	15	30
21	Karimganj	17	40
22	Karbi Anglong	75	143
23	North Cachar Hills	58	60
	Total	1,568	1,584

Source : Statistical Cell, Irrigation Department, Government of Assam.

The districtwise break up of completed schemes clearly shows clustering of minor schemes in the two districts of Nagaon and Kamrup. As on 31st March, 2001, number of total schemes set up in Nagaon district was 222 whereas those set up in Kamrup was 199. These two districts together accounted for about 26.85 per cent of total schemes completed in the state. The three districts of Barak Valley, viz. Cachar, Karimganj and Hailakandi accounted for only 3.38 per cent of the total schemes in the state. The list of ongoing schemes is also dominated by these two districts. Out of a total of 1584 ongoing schemes, as high as 15.66 per cent are in Nagaon district whereas Kamrup has a share of 9.97 per cent of the total schemes ongoing in the state. Clustering of minor schemes in these two districts may be because of a number of factors. These include participation of a large number of people in cultivation, awareness of the farmers regarding new technology in agriculture, good performance of the schemes and categories of cultivators engaged in agricultural activities etc.

3.3.2 (c) Development of Minor Irrigation Schemes in the Private Sector

A number of initiatives were taken under different agencies of the State Government to set up minor irrigation schemes in the private sector over the last two decades. The different agencies and departments of the government associated with installation of minor schemes in the state are Assam State Minor Irrigation Development Corporation (ASMIDC), the State Agricultural Department and Panchayat and Rural Development Department.

The Assam State Minor Irrigation Development Corporation was set up in 1980 and with the financial assistance from NABARD set up a number of shallow tube wells (STW) and low lift points (LLP). Till 1990-91, ASMIDC installed a total number of 49,800 STW and LLP. But after 1990-91, the Corporation failed to install even a single minor scheme due to lack of institutional finance.

The total number of minor schemes (mainly STWs) set up by the Department of Agriculture and Panchayat and Rural Development up to 1994-95 was 27,184 and 9,247 respectively. Since 1995-96, the Department of Agriculture has been implementing the World Bank assisted Programme "The Assam Rural Infrastructure and Agricultural Services Project" (ARIASP) which also has an irrigation sub-component. Under this project a total of 15,000 STWs were to be set up within a period of eight years. Later, the target was revised and the new target was installation of 41,150 numbers of STWs which in fact is 2.74 times of the initial estimate. For the financial year 1999-2000, the target was to install a total of 15,000 STWs which was successfully achieved. The progress of work under ARIASP across different districts over the years is shown in Table 3.8.

Table 3.8 : Districtwise Number of STWs Installed under ARIASP during Different Years

Sl. No.	*District*	*STWs installed during*		
		1997-98	*1998-99*	*1999-2000*
(1)	*(2)*	*(3)*	*(4)*	*(5)*
1.	Barpeta	456	900	1,300
2.	Bongaigaon	439	450	1,000
3.	Darrang	300	700	800
4.	Dhemaji	140	250	250
5.	Dhubri	698	1,400	1,300
6.	Dibrugarh	100	350	600
7.	Goalpara	392	750	800
8.	Golaghat	291	450	800
9.	Jorhat	122	300	850
10.	Kamrup	556	950	1,300
11.	Kokrajhar	100	200	300
12.	Lakhimpur	101	250	300
13.	Marigaon	258	650	1,000
14.	Nagaon	876	1,450	1,600
15.	Nalbari	308	800	800
16.	Sibsagar	200	300	700
17.	Sonitpur	283	950	600
18.	Tinsukia	130	200	700
	Total	5,750	11,500	15,000

Source : Executive Engineer, Directorate of Agriculture, Assam.

Total irrigation potential created up to the end of 1999-2000 was 64,500 hectares from the installation of a total of 32,250 tube-wells. The target for 2000-2001 was to create a potential of 30,000 hectares by installing a total of 15,000 shallow tube-wells.

Apart from the ARIASP programme, the State Agriculture Department has also been implementing a scheme called "Samriddha Krishak Yojana" (SKY) since the financial year 1999-2000. The basic objective of this scheme is to increase the area under irrigation for increasing the productivity and cropping intensity to bridge the gap between the production and requirement. Under this scheme, a group of farmers is provided with Shallow Tube Wells (STW) along with 5 H.P. pump sets. Preference is given to community and not to individuals and as such farmers are encouraged to organise Field Management Committee (FMC) which normally are provided with the pump sets. The scheme is sponsored by the National Bank for Agriculture and Rural Development (NABARD) under its programme of Rural Infrastructure Development Fund (RIDF) and in the first year of implementation of the scheme, a total of 30,000 STWs were set up in different districts of the state. For 2000-01, Agriculture Department had fixed a target of installation of 70,000 STWs in the state. Table 3.9 shows the districtwise distribution of STWs set up by the Department of Agriculture in the state under NABARD's RIDF scheme.

3.4 Irrigated Area in Relation to Net Sown Area

The physical progress of irrigation work in the state can be better understood if net sown area is also considered along with net irrigated area. As per data available, in 1997-98, net irrigated area in Assam was about 20.79 per cent of the net sown area as against the national average of 38.42 per cent. Even neighbouring eastern states like West Bengal and Orissa

Table 3.9 : Districtwise Distribution of STWs under SKY Scheme

Sl.No.	*District*	*No. of schemes*
(1)	*(2)*	*(3)*
1.	Kamrup	7,000
2.	Nalbari	5,000
3.	Kokrajhar	2,000
4.	Bongaigaon	4,000
5.	Darrang	6,000
6.	Sonitpur	5,000
7.	Lakhimpur	2,000
8.	Dhemaji	2,000
9.	Sibsagar	3,000
10.	Jorhat	3,000
11.	Golaghat	4,000
12.	Nagaon	15,000
13.	Morigaon	5,000
14.	Barpeta	5,500
15.	Dhubri	14,000
16.	Goalpara	5,000
17.	Dibrugarh	10,000
18.	Tinsukia	1,500
19.	Karbi Anglong	500
20.	Cachar	100
21.	Hailakandi	200
22.	Karimganj	200
	Total	1,00,000

Source : Executive Engineer, Directorate of Agriculture, Government of Assam.

had a much better figure than Assam at 34.97 per cent and 34.14 per cent respectively. Even in the North-East, Manipur had about 46.43 per cent of net sown area under irrigation. Thus development of irrigation in the state over the period of time has not been satisfactory. Table 3.10 shows net irrigated area of a few states of the country in relation to their net sown area for three different years.

Table 3.10 clearly shows that Assam has one of the lowest areas (net sown area) under irrigation. The figure has not only remained low but has also gone down over the period. From a percentage of 21.14 of irrigated area in 1991-92, the state had experienced a fall to 20.79 in 1997-98.

Table 3.10 : Net Irrigated Area of Different States as Percentage to Net Sown Area

States	*1991-92*	*1996-97*	*1997-98*
(1)	*(2)*	*(3)*	*(4)*
Andhra Pradesh	39.41	40.57	40.07
Assam	21.14	20.85	20.79
Haryana	76.00	76.21	76.84
Karnataka	21.55	21.91	23.45
Manipur	46.43	46.43	46.43
Orissa	30.52	35.02	34.14
Punjab	93.48	92.95	92.95
Tamil Nadu	45.50	52.72	52.77
Uttar Pradesh	64.17	68.66	68.59
West Bengal	34.89	34.98	34.97
India	35.24	38.61	38.42

Source: Agriculture, CMIE, November 2001.

3.5 Public Sector Investment in Irrigation

In 1996-97, the net state domestic product (NSDP) at current prices was Rs.16,81,148 lakh of which the share of agricultural NSDP was Rs. 6,58,691 lakh. Thus the contribution of agriculture to the state NSDP was 39.18 per cent. But the public sector investment on irrigation in the state is not much encouraging. In 1996-97, capital expenditure on irrigation at constant prices was Rs. 8,418 lakh which is about 5.67 per cent of the agricultural NSDP of the state for the year concerned. The percentage of public sector investment to the agricultural NSDP over the years has been found to be moderate. In 1980-81, investment on irrigation as percentage to the agricultural NSDP was 2.58 per cent which has gone up to 5.67 per cent in 1996-97. The share of public sector investment on irrigation to the agricultural NSDP of the state is given in Table 3.11.

It is evident from Table 3.11 that government investment made on irrigation as percentage to the state agricultural NSDP over the years has been hovering in between 2 -7 per cent.

Table 3.11 : Percentage Share of Public Sector Investment on Irrigation to Agricultural NSDP

Year	*Capital Expenditure on Irrigation (Rs. In lakhs)*	*Share of Investment on Irrigation to Agricultural NSDP*
(1)	*(2)*	*(3)*
1983-84	2,886	2.51
1984-85	4,802	4.45
1985-86	4,997	4.30
1986-87	6,175	5.56
1987-88	6,776	5.66
1988-89	4,704	3.98
1989-90	7,089	5.52
1990-91	7,146	5.47
1991-92	8,997	6.69
1992-93	7,380	5.44
1993-94	7,856	5.69
1994-95	8,495	5.95
1995-96	8,096	5.58
1996-97	8,418	5.67

Source : Finance Accounts of various years, Office of the Accountant General (A & E), Government of India, Guwahati and Directorate of Economics and Statistics, Government of Assam.

3.6 Government Irrigation and Water Charge

As per national policy, irrigation service charge has to be realised from the users of irrigation water in government schemes. The purpose behind this was to realise at least the operation and maintenance cost of the irrigation schemes. However, in case of Assam, rules regarding realisation of the levy have not been found to be consistent. The procedure to realise this water charge in the state continued till the later part of the 1970s. But after Janata Government came into power in the state, the provision of realising water tax was waived. However, Irrigation Department had levied this charge again in 1992 and the charge is to be realised on the basis of area irrigated. The cropwise rates for irrigation service charge in the state are shown in Table 3.12.

Table 3.12 : Crop-wise Irrigation Service Charges, 2000-01 (in Rupees)

Crop	Rate per bigha	Rate per hectare
(1)	(2)	(3)
1. Kharif	37.50	281.24
2. Wheat and other Rabi crops	75.00	562.50
3. Early ahu/ahu	100.00	751.00
4. Jute	20.00	150.00
5. Sugarcane	29.60	222.00

Source : Directorate of Economics and Statistics, Government of Assam.

3.7 Irrigation Potential Actually Created

The Department of Irrigation, Government of Assam has been following the definition of irrigation potential as given by the Planning Commission. According to this definition, irrigation potential is the gross area which can be irrigated from a project in a design year (1st July to 30th June of the succeeding year) for the projected cropping pattern and assumed water allowance on its full development. The gross irrigated area is the aggregate of the areas irrigated in different cropping seasons, the areas under two seasonal and perennial crops being counted only once in a year (Wade, 1976). In the following sections potential created under different departments has been analyzed.

3.7.1 Potential Created under Major/Medium and Government Minor Schemes

Although the Irrigation Department has been entrusted with the development of irrigation infrastructure in the state, a number of other government agencies/departments like ASMIDC, Department of Agriculture, Panchayat and Rural Development, etc. are also involved in setting up of irrigation schemes in the state. While the schemes set up by Department of Agriculture, ASMIDC, etc. are minor irrigation schemes, the Department of Irrigation has been implementing both minor and major/medium schemes. However, unlike the schemes of Department of Agriculture, the schemes under Irrigation Department are not handed over to the cultivators after their completion. According to the data available, the total potential created under major/medium and minor irrigation schemes under Department of Irrigation up to the end of March 2002 is 5,13,341 hectares of which 2,02,289 hectares, i.e. about 39.41 per cent are created under major/medium schemes and the rest 3,11,052 hectares, i.e. about 60.59 per cent are created under minor irrigation schemes. The potential created under government major/medium and minor irrigation schemes in the state from 1984-85[1] is shown in Table 3.13.

Table 3.13 : Sourcewise Irrigation Potential Created under Government Schemes in Different Years

(Area in hectares)

Year	*Major/Medium*	*Minor*	*Total Potential Created*
(1)	*(2)*	*(3)*	*(4)*
Up to 1984-85	1,05,543	2,10,169	3,15,712
1985-86	1,13,204	2,25,864	3,39,068
1986-87	1,33,896	2,40,254	3,74,150
1987-88	1,44,449	2,52,976	3,97,425
1988-89	1,48,298	2,60,616	4,08,914
1989-90	1,51,830	2,66,773	4,18,603
1990-91	1,53,880	2,72,139	4,26,019
1991-92	1,59,440	2,83,588	4,43,028
1992-93	1,64,993	2,90,657	4,55,650
1993-94	1,72,763	2,93,735	4,66,498
1994-95	1,79,273	2,97,738	4,77,011
1995-96	1,80,113	2,99,965	4,80,078
1996-07	1,80,113	3,00,477	4,80,590
1997-98	1,80,113	3,00,986	4,81,099
1998-99	1,81,789	3,03,245	4,84,034
1999-2000	1,88,489	3,06,953	4,95,442
2000-01	1,95,439	3,08,554	5,03,993
2001-02	2,02,289	3,11,052	5,13,341

Source : Statistical Cell, Irrigation Department, Government of Assam.

It is evident from Table 3.13 that potential created under minor schemes has always been more than that under major/ medium schemes. For example, up to 1984-85, potential created under minor schemes was about 66.57 per cent of the total potential created up to that year. Similarly for 2000-01, as against a share of 38.78 per cent under major/medium schemes, share of minor schemes in total potential created was 61.22 per cent. Thus potential created under minor schemes up to the year was about 1.58 times the potential created under major/medium schemes. As such, as pointed out by Dhawan (1997), the usage of the term 'minor' for these schemes does not clearly represent their importance in the irrigation scenario of the state as well.

3.7.2 Potential Created under Assam State Minor Irrigation Development Council (ASMIDC)

The total potential created under ASMIDC up to 1992-93 has been estimated at 1,49,205 hectares of which about 71.51 per cent is created by groundwater lift schemes and the rest 28.42 per cent by surface lift points. However, there has been no addition to the already created potential since 1992-93 because of shortage of fund. The potential created under ASMIDC in different years is given in Table 3.14.

3.7.3 Potential Created under the Departments of Agriculture and Panchayat and Rural Development

Till the end of 2001-02, the total potential created under the schemes set up by the Department of Agriculture is estimated at 3,36,284 hectares. This includes the potential created under the schemes of ARIASP and SKY apart from the already created potential. The total potential created by

Table 3.14 : Potential Created under ASMIDC in Different Years

(Area in hectares)

Year	*Potential Created Under*			*Total*
	Flow	*Lift*	*Ground water*	
(1)	*(2)*	*(3)*	*(4)*	*(5)*
1980-81	Nil	Nil	Nil	Nil
1981-82	Nil	240	3,810	4,050
1982-83	Nil	1,122	5,898	7,020
1983-84	Nil	3,933	11,859	15,792
1984-85	Nil	4,806	10,767	15,573
1985-86	Nil	3,867	6,885	10,752
1986-87	Nil	6,852	13,833	20,685
1987-88	Nil	7,950	15,255	23,205
1988-89	Nil	6,948	13,767	20,715
1989-90	Nil	3,318	11,256	14,574
1990-91	Nil	2,274	9,204	11,478
1991-92	Nil	1,095	3,732	4,827
1992-93	Nil	99	435	534
Total	Nil	42,504	1,06,701	1,49,205

Source : ASMIDC, Guwahati.

the schemes under Panchayat and Rural Development Department is estimated at 34,000 hectares. Thus the schemes under these two departments have created a total potential of 3,70,284 hectares which is about 35.85 per cent of the total potential created in the state up to 2001-02.

The gross irrigation potential created by the three government departments concerned with irrigation works of the state, viz. Irrigation, Agriculture and Panchayat and Rural Development and that of ASMIDC is shown in Table 3.15.

Table 3.15 clearly shows that irrigation coverage in the state is very low. Only about 38.25 per cent of the 27 lakh hectares of ultimate irrigation potential of the state has been covered by irrigation so far. Again, this figure constitutes only 25.82 per cent of about 40 lakh hectares gross cropped area of the state.

Table 3.15 : Gross Irrigation Potential Created in Assam up to 2001-02

(Area in hectares)

Department/ Agency	*Irrigation Potential Created up to 2000-01*		
	Major & Medium	*Minor*	*Total*
(1)	*(2)*	*(3)*	*(4)*
Irrigation Department	2,02,289	3,11,052	5,13,341
Agriculture Department	–	3,36,284	3,36,284
Panchayat and Rural Development Department	–	34,000	34,000
ASMIDC (up to 1992-93)	–	1,49,205	1,49,205
Total	2,02,289	8,30,541	10,32,830

Source : Statistical Cell, Irrigation Department, Government of Assam.

3.8 Utilisation of Irrigation Potential Created

Utilisation of irrigation potential created is an important aspect of irrigation schemes. The cropwise utilisation of irrigation potential created under government schemes is shown in Table 3.16.

The table shows that utilisation of created irrigation potential increased from 1,18,562.48 hectares in 1980-81 to 2,39,193.00 hectares in 1990-91. However, from 1991-92 it has been decreasing continuously till it reached its lowest at 1,13,088.16 in 1995-96. The drastic fall in utilisation during this period may be attributed to stopping of supply of electricity by the Assam State Electricity Board (ASEB) because of non-payment of dues by Irrigation Department. The situation, however, improved thereafter and in 2000-01, amount of utilisation of created irrigation potential was 1,14,731.81 hectares.

It is also evident from Table 3.16 that most of the utilisation has been taking place in the *kharif* season only which also shows the dominance of *kharif* crop in the state. In 1980-81, about 90.59 per cent of total utilisation was for *kharif* crops while for *rabi* and pre-*kharif* it was as meagre as

Table 3.16 : Cropwise Utilisation of Created Irrigation Potential in Different Years under Government Schemes

Year	*Irrigation Potential Utilised (Area in hectares)*		
	Kharif	*Rabi and Pre-Kharif*	*Total*
(1)	*(2)*	*(3)*	*(4)*
1980-81	1,07,406.83	11,155.65	1,18,562.48
1981-82	1,25,994.50	19,284.63	1,45,279.13
1982-83	1,39,704.47	18,221.05	1,57,925.52
1983-84	1,44,463.03	20,736.22	1,65,199.25
1984-85	1,51,046.66	21,065.33	1,72,111.99
1985-86	1,81,091.61	21,919.27	2,03,010.88
1986-87	2,00,499.70	25,257.46	2,25,757.16
1987-88	1,97,659.26	24,791.31	2,22,450.57
1988-89	1,95,936.83	39,394.19	2,35,331.02
1989-90	1,86,790.00	36,920.53	2,23,710.53
1990-91	2,01,175.00	38,018.00	2,39,193.00
1991-92	1,88,611.00	38,652.00	2,27,263.00
1992-93	1,86,955.00	27,967.00	2,14,922.00
1993-94	1,06,862.20	23,088.70	1,29,950.90
1994-95	1,30,958.57	16,290.07	1,47,248.64
1995-96	95,954.70	17,133.46	1.13,088.16
1996-97	1,00,140.19	13,959.88	1,14,100.07
1997-98	1,01,560.57	12,846.71	1,14,407.28
1998-99	1,00,152.42	15,773.94	1,15,926.36
1999-2000	97,984.27	21,237.42	1,19,221.69
2000-01	99,900.77	14,831.04	1,14,731.81

Source : Statistical Cell, Irrigation Department, Government of Assam.

9.41 per cent. The situation has not changed much over the years. In 1995-96, out of a total utilisation of 1,13,088.16 hectares, *kharif* crops alone accounted for 84.85 per cent leaving only 15.15 per cent for *rabi* and pre-*kharif* crops. Thus, for the whole period not much diversification of crops (in terms of utilisation by *rabi* and pre-*kharif* crops in total utilisation) has taken place.

Utilisation of irrigation potential as percentage of potential created in the state is also not very high. It is not only low but is also decreasing over the years. Table 3.17 shows the percentage of utilisation created under government sector in the state since 1984-85.

Table 3.17 : Percentage of Utilisation of Irrigation Potential Created during Different Years

Year	*Potential Created up to the Year (Area in hectares)*	*Potential Utilised During the Year (Area in hectares)*	*Percentage of Utilisation*
(1)	*(2)*	*(3)*	*(4)*
1984-85	3,15,712.00	1,72,111.99	54.52
1985-86	3,39,068.00	2,03,010.88	59.87
1986-87	3,74,150.00	2,25,757.16	60.34
1987-88	3,97,425.00	2,22,450.57	55.97
1988-89	4,08,914.00	2,35,331.02	57.55
1989-90	4,18,603.00	2,23,710.53	53.44
1990-91	4,26,019.00	2,39,193.00	56.15
1991-92	4,43,028.00	2,27,263.00	51.29
1992-93	4,55,650.00	2,14,922.00	47.17
1993-94	4,66,498.00	1,29,950.90	27.86
1994-95	4,77,011.00	1,47,248.64	30.87
1995-96	4,80,078.00	1,13,088.16	23.56
1996-97	4,80,590.00	1,14,100.07	23.74
1997-98	4,81,099.00	1,14,407.28	23.78
1998-99	4,84,034.00	1,15,926.36	23.95
1999-2000	4,95,442.00	1,19,221.69	24.06
2000-01	5,03.993.00	1,14,731.81	22.76

Source : Statistical Cell, Irrigation Department, Government of Assam.

It is clear from Table 3.17 that utilisation of potential created has been continuously decreasing over the years. For example, in 1984-85, the percentage of utilisation was 54.52 which rose to 60.34 in 1986-87. The rate then came down to 56.15 per cent in 1990-91 after some fluctuations in between. But since then there has been a gradual and continuous drop in the rate of utilisation and in 2000-01 it came down to as low as 22.76 per cent. This indicates that about 77 per cent of the potential created up to the year remained unutilised in the year. This is clearly gross underutilisation of created irrigation potential.

However, it can be reasonably assumed that irrigation potential created in a year is partly available for use in the same year, but wholly available for use in the next year.

Therefore, the percentage of utilisation as obtained in Table 3.17 may not be proper estimates of the rate of utilisation. As such percentage of utilisation has been estimated anew as given in Table 3.18. However, the estimated utilisation ratio is also not very high confirming that the utilisation of created irrigation potential under government irrigation schemes is not satisfactory.

Table 3.18 : Percentage of Utilisation of Irrigation Potential and Estimated Utilisation Ratio

Year	*Irrigation Potential Available at the end of the Year(in '000 hectares)*	*Potential Utilised during the Year (in '000 hectares)*	*Potential Utilised as per cent of Potential Available at the Beginning of the Year*	*Potential Utilised as per cent of Potential Available at the end of the Year*	*Estimated Utilisation Ratio (per cent)*
(1)	*(2)*	*(3)*	*(4)*	*(5)*	*(6)*
1984-85	315.712	172.112	—	59.52	—
1985-86	339.068	203.011	64.30	59.87	62.09
1986-87	374.150	225.757	66.58	60.34	63.42
1987-88	397.425	222.451	59.46	55.97	57.72
1988-89	408.914	235.331	59.21	57.55	58.38
1989-90	418.603	223.711	54.71	53.44	54.08
1990-91	426.019	239.193	57.13	56.15	56.64
1991-92	443.028	227.263	53.35	51.30	52.33
1992-93	455.650	214.922	48.51	47.17	47.84
1993-94	466.498	129.951	28.52	27.86	28.19
1994-95	477.011	147.249	31.56	30.87	31.22
1995-96	480.078	113.088	23.71	23.56	23.64
1996-97	480.590	114.100	23.77	23.74	23.76
1997-98	481.099	114.407	23.81	23.78	23.80
1998-99	484.034	115.926	24.10	23.95	24.03
1999-2000	495.442	119.222	24.63	24.06	24.35
2000-01	503.993	114.732	23.16	22.76	22.96

Source : Statistical Cell, Irrigation Department, Government of Assam.

3.9 Issues for Further Analysis

Notwithstanding the recent growth of irrigation capacity in the private sector, the development of irrigation infrastructure in the state over the years has taken place primarily under the government sector and government initiative. Public investment on irrigation has, however, remained at a moderate level of around 5 to 6 per cent of agricultural NSDP. Consequently, in spite of the abundance of both surface and groundwater resource, irrigation facility in the state has not got adequately developed. A serious concern in the irrigation sector of the state is the low rate of utilisation of created irrigation potential. About 67 per cent of the potential created in the state under government sector is found to remain unutilised during 2000-01. The huge amount of unutilised potential naturally calls for investigation to find out the factors responsible for low rate of utilisation. Macro level studies may not be sufficient to answer this particular question. To answer this we have to carry the investigations to the micro level. Moreover, introduction of irrigation facilities helps farmers to adopt new agricultural technology including use of HYVs, chemical fertilizers, pesticides, etc. This is the way to look at the effectiveness of irrigation schemes. Whether availability of irrigation water has been able to induce farmers to adopt this technology or not is another pertinent question associated with development of irrigation infrastructure in the state. So, an attempt has been made here to find out effectiveness of different irrigation schemes presently functioning in the state in terms of their capacity to induce farmers to adopt this new technology. Since macro studies are not enough to throw light on these aspects, carrying out fieldwork becomes important. Accordingly, a detailed field study was carried out in the year 2000-01 to investigate the twin problem of the utilisation and effectiveness of irrigation in Assam. The subsequent four chapters are based on the field study.

NOTE

1. It is worth mentioning that any study on irrigation of the state

is plagued by non-availability of adequate and reliable data. Information on area irrigated, sources of irrigation and irrigated area under different crops is not readily available and cannot be collected from a single source. Systematic data on irrigation in Assam are available only from 1980-81 onwards. The data relating to year prior to 1980-81 were based on *adhoc* estimates and are not comparable to the figures for the subsequent years.

REFERENCES

Bezbaruah, M. P. (1994), *Technological Transformation of Agriculture: A Study from Assam*, Mittal Publications, New Delhi.

Centre for Monitoring Indian Economy Pvt. Ltd. (2007), *Economic Intelligence Service : Agriculture*, April, Mumbai.

Das, M. M. (1984), *Peasant Agriculture in Assam*, Inter-India, New Delhi.

Dhawan, B. D. (1997), *India's Irrigation Sector—Myths and Realities*, Presidential Address, 57th Annual Conference of the Indian Society of Agricultural Economics held at Govind Ballabh Pant University of Agriculture and Technology, Pantnagar, December. 29-31 (Mimeo).

Goswami, A. (1992), "Some Constraints of Economic Development of Assam" in Saikia, P. D. and Borah, Durgeswar (Eds.) *Constraints of Economic Development in N. E. India*, Omsons Publications, New Delhi and Guwahati.

Goswami, D. C. (1989), "Floods and their Impact on Agriculture in Assam" in Goswami, P. C. (ed.) *Agriculture in Assam*, Assam Institute of Development Studies, Guwahati.

Government of Assam (2002), *Economic Survey*, Directorate of Economics and Statistics, Guwahati-781006, Assam.

Government of Assam (2006), *Statistical Hand Book Assam*, Directorate of Economics and Statistics, Guwahati-781006, Assam.

Government of India (1995), *Annual Report*, Ministry of Water Resources, Government of India.

Roy, Niranjan and Bezbaruah, M. P. (2002), *Agricultural Growth and Regional Economic Development*, Mittal Publications, New Delhi.

Sharma, P. (1992), *A Study of Irrigation Development and Its Impact on Food Grains Production in Assam*, Ph. D.Dissertation submitted to Gauhati University.

Wade, Robert (1976), Performance of Irrigation Projects, *Economic and Political Weekly*, January 17, p. 64.

4

Field Study Location, Sampling Design and the Sample

4.1 The Purpose of Field Study

The discussions in chapter 3 on the state of agriculture and irrigation in Assam are based on aggregate data about the agriculture sector of the state collected from various government and semi-government sources. The problems of agriculture and irrigation in the state have been analysed in the chapter from a macro standpoint by looking into the performance of the agriculture sector as a whole. Yet as noted in the concluding part of chapter 3, the macro level analysis fails to provide answers to many pertinent questions such as whether difference in ownership and form of irrigation schemes affect the efficiency in utilisation and effectiveness in productive use of irrigation of the schemes in the state. There may be several institutional, socio-economic, technological and management related factors at the ground level, which might have restrained fuller utilisation of created irrigation potential and effective use of irrigation by farmers. To obtain answers to such questions, it was felt necessary to carry out detailed investigation at the micro level.

Accordingly, a field survey was carried out during the winter of 2000-01 at a few selected areas of the state.

The field study was aimed at the identification of factors affecting performance of different types of irrigation schemes in the state. The performance had been examined basically on two counts. One is efficiency in utilisation of installed irrigation potential and the other is effectiveness of different irrigation forms in inducing farmers in using productivity enhancing practices.

4.2 Selection of Area for Field Study

The field study locations were selected from the Brahmaputra Valley which constitutes 72 per cent of area and 92 per cent of population in the state. The other two geographical divisions, namely the Barak Valley and the Hills were left out as irrigation potential developed in these areas is still very limited. Hence the problem of underutilisation of installed irrigation potential is somewhat less relevant in these regions. To make the field study representative, three districts from three different agro-climatic zones falling in upper, middle and lower reach of the Brahmaputra Valley have been selected as the broad locations of the field study. These districts are Dibrugarh in Upper Brahmaputra Valley Zone, Nagaon in Central Brahmaputra Valley Zone and Barpeta in Lower Brahmaputra Valley Zone. The selection of the districts is guided by the fact that these districts have better concentration of irrigation schemes in terms of number and variety, especially of government owned schemes.

4.3 Selection of Schemes under Government Sector and Collection of Data

The method adopted for selecting the schemes under field study area is the purposive sampling method. Out of the

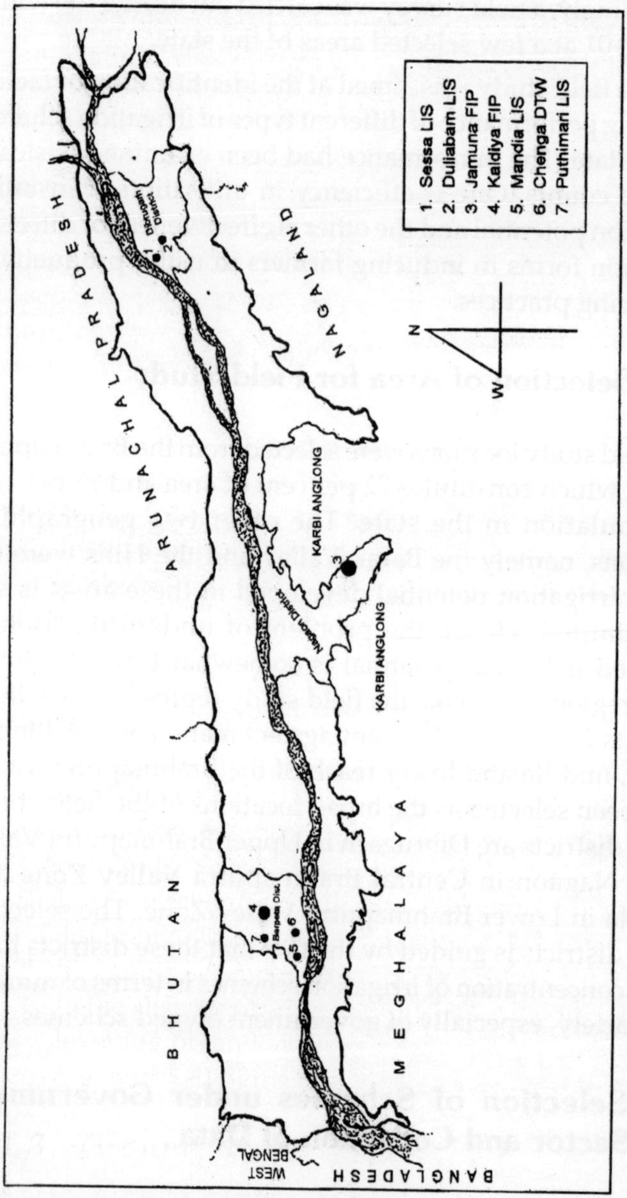

Fig 4.1 : Brahmaputra Valley Showing Broad Field Study Locations and Included Government Schemes.

two major schemes completed so far in the state, Jamuna Irrigation Project was selected for field study. This scheme is the oldest of all the major and medium irrigation schemes in the state and also the largest in terms of area coverage. So, selection of this scheme for fieldwork was an automatic one. As for medium category, different considerations had to be taken into account. From a total of 8 completed and 5 ongoing schemes, Kaldiya Irrigation Scheme from Barpeta district was selected for field study. Because of maximum concentration of medium schemes in Barpeta district and also its location in the Lower Brahmaputra Valley zone, it was quite natural to include one scheme from this district. Although there are quite a few schemes of this category in the district, Kaldiya was selected because of its better accessibility and law and order situation compared to the other schemes in the district.

For government minor schemes, about 15 to 20 per cent of the total functioning schemes of the districts were taken for fieldwork. Care was taken to include variety of schemes, viz. surface lift, ground water lift, surface flow etc. so as to make comparative discussion between different categories of schemes. Thus, Sessa and Duliabam from a total of 8 functioning schemes were selected from Dibrugarh district and three schemes from Barpeta district, viz. Mandia, Puthimari and Chenga were selected from a total of 23 functioning schemes in the district. Here Sessa, Duliabam and Mandia are surface lift schemes where water is lifted with the help of barge from rivers while in case of Puthimari water is lifted from *beel*. Chenga is a deep tube-well scheme in Barpeta district. Further details of the government schemes included in the field study are given in Appendix 4.A to this chapter.

Data for field investigation under government irrigation have been collected from two types of sources. The first type of source is the officials of Irrigation Department of respective projects from whom necessary information were collected through interview method. The second type of source is the farmers in command areas of the projects from whom data were collected using a structured questionnaire. The sample of farmers in command area for the purpose of data collection was selected by using a two stage random sampling design.

In each scheme the villages constituted the primary sample units, and the farm households were the secondary and ultimate sampling units. In case of major and medium schemes, first of all, the lists of the beneficiary villages were collected and from that two or three villages were selected at random. Care was taken to see that villages selected adequately represent the different reaches of the scheme concerned. In case of minor schemes, however, this did not create much problem because the areas of operation of these schemes are fairly small. In the second stage, about 10 to 12 per cent of farm households in each selected village were taken at random for collection of data on different aspects of farm operations and use of irrigation water.

4.4 The Sampling Design for Private Minor Schemes

For comparability, the sample of farm households under privately owned schemes has been drawn from the same three districts, namely Dibrugarh, Nagaon and Barpeta to which the government owned schemes studied belong. The sample from each of the three districts was selected using a three stage sampling design. In the first stage, two Agricultural Extension Officers (A.E.O.) Circles were purposively selected on the consideration of having sizeable concentration of privately owned shallow tube-wells for irrigation. In the next stage, one village each from each of these circles was selected. Finally, about 15 to 20 per cent of irrigated farms were selected at random as the ultimate sample units. Responses from sample farmers were recorded using a structured questionnaire.

4.5 Sample Profile and their Agrarian Structure

In the following few sections an attempt has been made to analyse the composition of the samples and their agrarian structure like size of operational holding, incidence of tenancy, etc.

4.5.1 Composition of the Sample

In the field survey conducted in different parts of the state, a total of 172 farmers selected were interviewed. The names of the villages and the number of sample farms included are given in Tables 4.1 and 4.2.

Table 4.1 : Survey Locations with Number of Sample Farms under Government Sector

Scheme/Village	*Number of Farm Households Selected for Field Study*
(1)	*(2)*
A. Major/Medium Scheme	**51**
A1. Jamuna/Kaki	10
A2. Jamuna/Buragaon	10
A3. Jamuna/Donkygaon	11
A4. Kaldiya/Daisingri	10
A5. Kaldiya/Tuplai Panbari	10
B. Minor Schemes	**54**
B1. Sessa	12
B2. Duliabam	10
B3. Mandia	12
B4. Puthimari	10
B5. Chenga	10
Total (A + B)	**105**

Table 4.2 : Survey Locations with Number of Sample Farms under Private Irrigation

District/ Village	*Number of Farm Households Selected for Field Study*
(1)	*(2)*
A. Dibrugarh	**22**
A1. Dihing Thekerani (Mancotta)	11
A2. Panigaon Kalakhowa (Barbaruah)	11
B. Nagaon	**24**
B1. Katimari Grant (Chakalaghat)	12
B2. Gotonga (Samaguri)	12
C. Barpeta	**21**
C1. Keotkuchi (Keotkuchi)	11
C2. Domoni (Barpeta Road)	10
Total (A + B + C)	**67**

Note : Names of respective A.E.O Circles are given in parentheses.

The sample includes 105 farm households from government schemes and 67 from private schemes. Category-wise, out of a total of 172 samples, 51 were from major and medium schemes and 121 were from minor schemes which again comprise 54 from government schemes and 67 from private sector. The composition of the samples according to form and ownership is given in Table 4.3.

Table 4.3 : Composition of the Samples According to Form and Ownership

Form Ownership	*Major/Medium*	*Minor*	*Total*
(1)	*(2)*	*(3)*	*(4)*
Government Sector	51	54	105 (61.05)
Private Sector	Nil	67	67 (30.95)
Total	51 (29.65)	121 (71.35)	172 (100.00)

Note : Figures in parentheses represent percentages of total sample.

Table 4.3 shows that 61.05 per cent of the total samples are taken from government schemes and 30.95 per cent are from private schemes. According to technical nature, major and medium schemes constitute 29.65 per cent of the total samples while samples under minor schemes constitute the rest 71.35 per cent.

4.5.2 The Size of Operational Holdings

The distribution of the sample farms according to the size of their operational holdings is shown in Table 4.4.

Table 4.4 : Distribution of Sample Farms According to Size of Operational Holdings under Different Categories of Schemes

Size Class of Operational Holding (hectares)	*Government*		*Private*	*Total*
	Major/Medium	*Minor*		
(1)	*(2)*	*(3)*	*(4)*	*(5)*
Below 0.5	0 (0.00)	2 (3.70)	1 (1.49)	3 (1.74)
0.5 to 1.00	4 (7.84)	8 (14.81)	6 (8.96)	18 (10.47)
1.00 to 2.00	16 (31.37)	31 (57.41)	16 (23.88)	63 (36.63)
2.00 to 3.00	17 (33.33)	12 (22.22)	22 (32.84)	51 (29.65)
3.00 to 5.00	11 (21.57)	0 (0.00)	14 (20.90)	25 (14.53)
5.00 to 8.00	3 (5.88)	1 (1.85)	7 (10.45)	11 (6.40)
Above 8.00	0 (0.00)	0 (0.00)	1 (1.49)	1 (0.58)
Total	51 (100.00)	54 (100.00)	67 (100.00)	172 (100.00)

Note : Figures in parentheses represent percentages of column totals.

Table 4.4 shows that the maximum concentration of sample farms is in the size category of 1.00 to 2.00 hectares which accounts for about 36.63 per cent of the total farms. This is followed by the size category of 2.00 to 3.00 hectares contributing about 29.65 per cent of the total sample farms. These two size groups together account for about 66.28 per cent of the operational holdings under the samples. The figures in the Table 4.4 also show that 84 out of 172, that is about 49 per cent of sample farmers have operational holdings below 2.0 hectares. Only 11 farmers have operational holdings between 5.0 to 8.0 hectares which is about 6.4 per cent of the total operational holdings. The proportion of marginal farms in the sample is relatively small; it being only 12.21 per cent of the total operational holding. Only 12 farms, i.e. 6.98 per cent of the total farms have operational holding of size more than 5 hectares while about 14.53 per cent of the farms have holding of size category 3.00 to 5.00 hectares.

While the government minor schemes follow the pattern followed by all the farms taken together, major/medium and private minor schemes follow a slightly different pattern so far as distribution of farms under different categories are concerned. In both these categories of schemes, the maximum concentration of farms is found in the size category of 2.00 to 3.00 hectares followed by the size category of 1.00 to 2.00 hectares. While there is no farm in the size category of above 8 hectares in case of major/medium and government minor schemes, there is 1 farm representing 1.49 per cent of total farms under private minor schemes in the said category.

The combined area of all 172 operational holdings comes to 406.49 hectares which indicates that the average size of operational holdings of the sample farmers under different categories of irrigation schemes was 2.36 hectares. This size of operational holding for the sample farmers is higher than the average size of operational holding for the state as a whole at 1.31 hectares. This may be attributed to the fact that in our case only the farms using irrigation water have been considered and for effective operation of farms under irrigated conditions the size of operational holding should be sufficiently large. Area under different size class of holdings under various types of schemes is shown in Table 4.5.

Table 4.5 : Area under Different Size Class of Holdings under Various Types of Schemes

(*In hectares*)

Size Class of Operational Holding	*Government*		*Private*	*Total*
	Major/Medium	*Minor*		
(1)	*(2)*	*(3)*	*(4)*	*(5)*
Below 0.5	0 (0.00)	0.87 (1.01)	0.47 (0.24)	1.34 (0.33)
0.5 to 1.00	2.81 (2.22)	6.23 (7.26)	5.15 (2.64)	14.19 (3.48)
1.00 to 2.00	24.63 (19.43)	44.31(51.63)	24.23 (12.44)	93.17 (22.88)
2.00 to 3.00	41.23 (32.53)	28.65 (33.38)	53.01 (27.23)	122.89 (30.17)
3.00 to 5.00	38.95 (30.73)	0 (0.00)	53.4 (27.43)	92.35 (22.67)
5.00 to 8.00	19.14 (15.10)	5.76 (6.71)	44.39 (22.80)	69.29 (17.01)
Above 8.00	0 (0.00)	0 (0.00)	14.06 (7.22)	14.06 (3.45)
Total	126.76 (100.00)	85.82 (100.00)	194.71 (100.00)	407.29 (100.00)

Note : Figures in parentheses represent percentages of column total.

The largest share of operational area (30.17 per cent) covered in the field study is from the size class of 2.00 to 3.00 hectares. This is closely followed by size categories of 1.00 to 2.00 hectares and 3.00 to 5.00 hectares accounting for about 22.88 per cent and 22.67 per cent respectively of the total area under all operational holdings. The area of the marginal farms taken together constitutes only about 3.81 per cent of the total area under all farms.

4.5.3 Incidence of Tenancy among Sample Farmers

The details of distribution of tenant farmers are shown in Table 4.6. The table shows that 80 out of 172, that is, about 46.51 per cent of sample farmers, have land on lease as part of their operational holdings. But in 25 per cent of 80 cases of tenancy, land leased in constitutes more than half of the farmers' operational holdings. In case of only 8.75 per cent of tenant farmers even 75 per cent or more of operational

Table 4.6 : Distribution of Tenant Farmers in the Sample according to the Percentage of Leased Area in their Operational Holdings

Percentage of Leased Area in Operational Holdings	*Total Number of Tenant Farmers*
(1)	*(2)*
Below 25	23 (28.75)
25 to 50	37(46.25)
50 to 75	13(16.25)
75 and above	7(8.75)
Total	80(100.00)

Note : Figures in the parentheses represent percentage of the total sample.

holdings were found to be leased in land. In 2 cases, i.e. 2.5 per cent of total samples, the leased in land constitutes the whole of the operational holdings of the sample farms.

The schemewise distribution of tenant farmers according to proportion of leased area in their operational holding is given in Table 4.7.

Table 4.7 : Schemewise Distribution of Tenant Farmers in the Sample according to the Percentage of Leased Area in their Operational Holdings.

Percentage of Leased Area in Operational Holding	*Number of Tenant Farmers in Government*		*Private*	*Total*
	Major/Medium	*Minor*		
(1)	*(2)*	*(3)*	*(4)*	*(5)*
Below 25	6 (26.09)	5 (27.78)	11 (28.21)	22 (27.5)
25 to 50	10 (43.48)	9 (50.00)	20 (51.28)	39 (48.75)
50 to 75	5 (21.74)	2 (11.11)	5 (12.82)	12 (15.00)
75 and above	2 (8.70)	2 (11.11)	3 (7.69)	7 (8.75)
Total	23 (100.00)	18 (100.00)	39 (100.00)	80 (100.00)

Table 4.7 shows that 39 out of 67 farm households under private schemes, i.e. 58 per cent have leased in land as part of their operational holding. The figure is relatively low for

farms under government irrigation where 39.05 per cent of farm households have leased in land. In 21 per cent of 39 cases of tenancy under private schemes, land leased in constitutes more than half of the farmer's operational holdings. The corresponding figure for all the schemes taken together comes out to be 24 per cent. On the whole, about 20.56 per cent of the combined operational holdings in the sample area are found to be under tenancy.

Tenancy is found to be temporary, usually of one year and also completely informal. The mode of payment of rent is not found to be uniform in all cases. Traditional system of share cropping is prevalent in a large number of tenant farmers in the sample areas. The mode of payment in such cases is to share output between the tenant and the landlord, usually at 50 : 50 ratio with or without sharing of cost by the landlord. However, with availability of irrigation water tenancy on fixed rent basis has also emerged in the sample areas. In such cases, sample farmers are found to take land on lease for growing non-rice crops, mainly vegetables with irrigation.

APPENDIX 4.A

The Government Irrigation Schemes included in the Field Study

Considering the objectives of the study and nature of irrigation work in the state, a variety of schemes had to be included in the field study. These include lift and flow schemes under government sector, shallow tube wells under private sector, etc. In the following section, we present brief backgrounds for all the schemes selected for field study.

4. A.1. Jamuna Irrigation Project

The Jamuna Irrigation Project is the first medium flow irrigation venture in Assam, located primarily in the southern part of Nagaon District. It is a run of the river diversion system commissioned in 1969 with a culturable command area of 27,705.66 hectares. The project was designed to create the irrigation potential to a gross command area of 30,996 hectares. It is designed to tap the water resources of Jamuna river near Bakuliaghat by construction of Main Weir, Head Regulator, and Guide Bunds, which facilitated the diversion of the river flow to the canal system. The project has a canal network of 264.63 km with 3 (three) major distributaries and a number of minors, sub-minors and water courses.

The project report was initially prepared by Central Water and Power Commission (CWPC) in 1959-60 after carrying out survey in the region where the project is implemented. Besides the CWPC, The Geological Survey of India carried out geological study and the Directorate of River Research Station, State PWD (Flood Control and Irrigation Department) carried out soil exploration of the headworks site. The model study of the headworks was designed by the Central Water and Power Research Station, Poona in 1964.

The final survey and design of the canal system was carried out by the State Engineers of the PWD (Flood Control & Irrigation Department).

The project was approved by the Government of India for inclusion in the Third Five Year Plan. Actual work of the project was started from January 1965 and completed in May 1969. However, although physically completed and irrigation was made available to cultivators, full development of facilities was envisaged only after 5 years of completion of works, that is, by bringing 20 per cent of the area under irrigation every year.

The present Jamuna Irrigation Project was formulated in the year 1960-61 and concurrence of Government of India was communicated by Planning Commission's letter no. Nr-14 (7)/61, dt. 17.3.62 for an estimated cost of Rs. 19.23 million. The original estimate was subsequently revised and concurred by Government of India for Rs. 39.60 million in 1969. The expenditure as against the sanctioned estimate is reported to be Rs. 43.43 million.

4.A.1.1 The Headwork

The headwork at Bakuliaghat consisted of the main weir, head regulator and guide bunds to facilitate diversion of water to the main canal without the provision of storage. The main canal is 4.2 km long and the discharge capacity is 700 cusec. The canal system network was framed with 3 (three) main distributaries D_1, D_2 and D_3 from the main canal. With the main canal distributaries, minors, sub-minors and the water courses of about 264.63 kms. of canal network was constructed to irrigate the entire command.

4.A.1.2 Establishment of CADA

Government of India selected the Jamuna Irrigation Project

for the extensive works of Command Area Development Programme in 1976-77. The decision was supported by successful completion and operation of the pilot project in the command area. As a result, in 1983-84, the CADA was set up at Katimari, Nagaon district Table 4.A.1 and 4.A.2 show the yearwise expenditure on CAD Activities and allotment expenditure on maintenance fund for Jamuna CAD Division.

Table 4.A.1 : Yearwise Breakup of Expenditure on CAD Activities of Jamuna Irrigation Project

(*Rs. In lakhs*)

Year	*Establishment*	*Works*	*Total*
(1)	*(2)*	*(3)*	*(4)*
1978-79	2.78	0.93	3.71
1979-80	3.80	0.12	5.92
1980-81	5.72	4.76	10.48
1981-82	6.06	31.78	37.84
1982-83	7.94	24.74	32.68
1983-84	11.58	14.65	206.22
1984-85	12.77	34.81	47.58
1985-86	15.45	71.78	87.23
1986-87	19.00	80.35	99.35
1987-88	22.21	172.36	194.57
1988-89	25.96	158.39	184.35
1989-90	31.69	225.87	257.56
1990-91	39.00	222.83	261.83
1991-92	43.805	218.086	261.891
1992-93	46.64	115.272	161.912
1993-94	29.788	110.435	140.223
1994-95	72.08	50.50	131.58
1995-96	90.17	55.29	145.46
1996-97	121.48	37.20	158.68
1997-98	140.22	14.00	167.14
1998-99	103.12	16.57	129.69
1999-2000	46.12	38.68	84.80
2000-01 up to June 2000	7.72	5.22	12.94

Source : CADA, Jamuna, Hojai.

Table 4.A.1 shows that expenditure on CAD activities has come down significantly in the decade of 1990s.

Table 4.A.2 : Yearwise Allotment and Expenditure of Maintenance Fund for Jamuna CAD Division Irrigation

Year	*Fund Allotted during the Year (Rs. in lakhs)*	*Expenditure Incurred during the Year (Rs. in lakhs)*
(1)	*(2)*	*(3)*
1976-77	Nil	Nil
1977-78	Nil	Nil
1978-79	16.018	15.949
1979-80	11.688	11.049
1980-81	19.240	19.342
1981-82	21.021	21.013
1982-83	18.666	18.568
1983-84	29.636	29.785
1984-85	31.773	31.774
1985-86	44.166	44.166
1986-87	49.867	49.882
1987-88	45.591	49.591
1988-89	35.660	37.293
1989-90	19.475	23.929
1990-91	12.00	24.224
1991-92	9.75	33.199
1992-93	11.17	23.59
1993-94	16.54	26.547
1994-95	7.93	22.84
1995-96	3.50	26.33
1996-97	4.15	23.67
1997-98	3.51	24.45
1998-99	3.00	37.07
1999-2000	52.15	52.14
2000-01 up to June 20	19.40	12.62

Source : CADA, Jamuna, Hojai

It is evident from Table 4.A.2 that allotment of fund for maintenance of the Project has also come down in the recent years. However, allotment of fund in the year 1999-2000 has been found to be quite good.

4.A.1.3 The Canal System

From the headwork at Bakuliaghat, the river water is diverted to the main canal. The designed capacity of the main canal is

700 cusec and its length is 4.24 km. The main canal delivers water to 3 (three) distributaries D_1, D_2 and D_3. The total command of the distributary D_1 and its minors and sub-minors is 8,754 hectares. The command area of the canal system of D_2 is 7,945 hectares and that of D_3 is 9,354 hectares. In addition to the minors and the sub-minors other water courses and subsidiaries are also constructed in many places to meet up the demand of the farmers.

4.A.1.4 The Jamuna River

The Jamuna Irrigation Project provides water in the field by tapping the water of river Jamuna, a major tributary of the Kopili. Jamuna river has its origin in the Karbi Hills. From its origin to Bakuliaghat the slope of the river is very steep with a number of rapids and falls. From Bakuliaghat to its confluence with the Kopili river, it flows in the plains of Nagaon district. The main tributaries are Dimoru Nala on the left and the Dikhari Nala, on the right side. The total length of the river is 131.2 km. and it covers an area of 3,960 sq. km.

4.A.1.5 Physical Features of the Command Area

The command area of the project is bounded by the river Jamuna on the north and by the Kapili river on the south and south-west. The Dimoru Nala, which is a tributary of the Jamuna River, runs through the command area. The Dimoru and the Jamuna flow approximately in the east-west direction. There are some fairly big villages but no town in the command area.

4.A.1.6 Expenditure Incurred in the Works Done

The total estimated cost of the project is Rs. 396.90 lakhs up to 1968-69. Taking into account the expenditure incurred under the plan and normal budget, etc., total expenditure for the project comes to Rs.698.58 lakhs up to the year 1972-73. Out of this amount Rs.422.95 lakhs was incurred for construction of the weir, regulators etc. against the provision of Rs.225.12 lakhs.

4.A.2 Kaldiya Irrigation Project

The Kaldiya Irrigation Project is a medium project on the river Kaldiya in Barpeta district. The project was envisaged with a view to bringing under command an area which needs irrigation on a priority basis. The crop production in the area was insufficient as the pattern of rainfall was erratic and occasional drought also told upon the crop production. The project report hoped that "the scheme on implementation will serve as protection against occasional drought and will promote multiple cropping which hitherto could not be achieved without artificial irrigation." It was proposed to construct a barrage across the river Kaldiya near Rehabari in Barpeta district to tap about 10 cusec of water for perennial irrigation scheme.

The river Kaldiya originates from the Himalayan foothills south of Bhutan between elevation 3000 ft-4000 ft (approx) and flows towards south-west to meet the river Daijama in the north Doomni T.E. It has a steep fall of the order of 300′-400′ per mile in the foothills. Like most of the rivers on the northern bank of the Brahmaputra, the river has wide and shallow channels with steep bed grade immediately below the foothills where they meander and flow down with a flatter bed grade. The river in the upper reach is about 150′-200' in width and contains mainly river boulders.

After meeting the river Daijama, it flows towards the south through the villages Rehabari, Golagaon, Akaya, Kochmari, Gandhligaon, Jalahghat, Bhaluki, etc. to meet the river Tihu. The river Dekadong meets the Kaldiya near village Bhebla. It then flows further south to meet the river

Nakhanda near Barpeta town. In lower reach the river is shallow and the bed consists of small pebbles.

The Kaldiya irrigation project was started with an estimated cost of Rs.811.15 lakh to provide water to an estimated area of 16,500 hectares. The entire command area of the scheme falls under erstwhile Kamrup district (now Barpeta district) and is bounded between latitude 26°-27′ and 26°-37′and longitude 91°-8′ and 91°-15′.

The location of the weir is in Rehabari village under Bajali sub-division of Barpeta district. The main canal takes off from the right bank of the weir and the total length of the main canal is 23.351 km. There are 8 (eight) branch canals which take off from the main canal. The total length of the minor and branch canals are 35.425 km.

Provisions for field channel carrying discharge below one cusec was to be made by the public by construction of water courses which will be constructed by Irrigation Department under Command Area Development Programme. The estimated cost of Kaldiya Irrigation Scheme as per first project was Rs. 179.57 lakhs which was approved by Planning Commission in June 1974. The first project report was prepared in the year 1972-73 and the schedule of estimate for all the concerning items of works was accordingly prepared based on costing to 1972-73 as base year. After doing the preliminary arrangement on receipt of approval, the work was actually started from 1975-76. Initially it was proposed that the work would be completed within three years from the work of commencement, but unfortunately it took about two decades for the completion of the project. The first revised project report of the scheme duly took note of this and tried to explain the delay in the proceedings by relating it to the escalation of cost of different construction materials.

4.A.3. Sessa LIS

It is one of the few functioning minor schemes in Dibrugarh

district. Located near Gamon bridge under Barbaruah Development Block the scheme is a surface lift irrigation scheme. Water is lifted from river Buridihing with the help of electric motors and is distributed through a main canal. Started in the year 1975-76 at an initial investment of 7.98 lakhs, the scheme took about 9 years for providing water to the field and was completed in 1984-85. The total installed capacity of the scheme was 930 hectares which includes 600 hectares for *kharif* and 330 hectares for *rabi*. The villages included under the command area of the scheme are Kotoha, Kotoha Borbil, Kotoha Nagaon and Kotoha Bengali Gaon.

4.A.4 Duliabam LIS

The scheme is a lift irrigation scheme and is situated on river Dimow in village Dulia under Khowang Development Block. Water is lifted from the river with the help of 3 (three) electric motors of 20 HP each and is distributed through a main canal and a branch canal. Originally, the scheme had 5 electric pumps out of which only 3 are functioning now. The original length of the main canal was 2500 metres which was extended later on by another 1500 metres. Similarly, the branch canal was originally 1320 metres of length and was extended by another 1000 metres later on. Initiated in the year 1971-72 at an initial investment of Rs. 22.2 lakhs, the scheme was completed in the year 1973-74. The total potential created is 135 hectares out of which Net Irrigable Area (NIA) is 105 hectares. The command area of the scheme consists of three villages, namely Duliabam, Dulia Lahowal and 11/164 ORR Grant. The scheme was renovated during 1999-2000 and currently the scheme is functioning well.

4.A.5 Mandia LIS

Out of a total 11 completed minor irrigation schemes in Barpeta subdivision of the district, Mandia LIS is a functioning scheme. The scheme has two extensions—extension old and extension new. Extension old has two points at Bhatkuchi while extension new has one point at Kopoha. Kopoha point of Mandia LIS was taken for field study. The scheme is a river water based surface lift scheme and water is lifted from river Bhelengi (also known as Pahumara) with the help of a barge. The river is a perennial one, and so there is no difficulty in lifting water during winter too. Started in the financial year 1981-82, the scheme initially had three motors on running of which total potential created amounted to around 200 hectares. But at present only 2 motors are in running condition. Because of shortage of fund for maintenance, the government has stopped looking after the scheme. The day to day maintenance and minor repairing of the scheme have now been left to the Field Management Committee (FMC) of the village which was formed in the year 1987-88. The scheme is now burdened with a number of problems which has resulted in reduction of the command area of the scheme. The problems affecting the scheme include, among others, mechanical defect, broken canal structure, lack of maintenance, etc. The command area of the scheme is a low-lying one which is flooded by the water of river Pahumara during summer. The farmers, therefore, cannot raise more than one crop. Summer paddy is the main crop practised in the command area. HYV seeds are extensively used by the farmers and the popular varieties used include TTB, Pusa, Mahnsuri, etc. The yield of paddy in the area is very good. It ranges between 40-45 quintal per hectare. Use of chemical fertilizer and other inputs of new technology are most common in the area. Soil lining, use of pesticides are also done by the farmers. All the benefited farmers under the command area are of immigrant origin including both Hindus and Muslims.

4.A.6 Chenga DTW

This DTW scheme is located under Chenga Development

Block in Barpeta district. Presently two points of the scheme are functioning, one at Khongra and the other at Musalmanpara. Out of these two, the point at Musalmanpara was taken up for fieldwork. The beneficiaries of the scheme include both indigenous and immigrant Muslims. The estimated potential of the scheme is 60 hectares.

4.A.7 Puthimari LIS

It is another functioning surface lift minor irrigation scheme in Barpeta district. The scheme is situated in a village called Puthimari under Gobardhana Development Block about 4 km. towards east of Sorbhog town. The scheme was started in the year 1987 at an estimated cost of Rs. 7,85,000.00 and was completed in the year 1989. The scheme consists of 2 (two) pumps of 20 HP each. Water is lifted from a *beel* called Sorbhog *beel* in village Puthimari with the help of these two pumps and water is carried to the field through a main canal. There is no branch canal of the scheme. The potential of the scheme was estimated at 40 hectares of gross cropped area (GCA). The cropping pattern of the area is dominated by winter paddy. Vegetables are also grown in substantial quantities. Other notable crops raised in the area include wheat, pulses, oilseeds and autumn paddy.

5

Utilisation and Effectiveness of Irrigation under Different Conditions

In the previous chapter the profile of the sample farms including the agrarian structure of the sample farmers has been presented. That is followed up in this chapter by a comparative analysis of utilisation of irrigation potential and extent of use of better farming practices by sample farmers under different conditions of irrigation. Though the ratios and averages for this analysis have been computed separately for different sample locations and irrigation projects, the main thrust of comparison is between the efficiency in utilisation and effectiveness in using better farming practices under government owned schemes and private schemes.

5.1 The Utilisation Rate

For comparison of efficiency in utilisation in different schemes, utilisation rate has been calculated separately for government and private irrigation schemes. However, the method used for calculation of this rate is different for the two types of schemes. Since the information regarding potential created and gross area irrigated could be obtained from secondary source for each of the government schemes, the rate of utilisation of these schemes is based on gross area irrigated. The utilisation rate, in this context, is defined as the ratio of gross area irrigated from the scheme to annually irrigable area under the scheme expressed as percentage. Overall utilisation rate for schemes under government sector is calculated by taking a weighted average of sample utilisation rates under major/medium and minor irrigation schemes, the weight being the share of these two types of irrigation schemes in total potential created under government schemes. This has to be done as the number of sample schemes under government major/medium and minor is very few and thus proportionate representation (numberwise) has not been possible. The information on annual irrigable area for the private shallow tube well (STW) based schemes could not be ascertained. Therefore, the utilisation rate had to be computed using data on net area irrigated and net irrigable area. The net irrigable area of any STW scheme has been assumed to be 2 hectares per STW as reported by the Department of Agriculture, Government of Assam. The utilisation rate for STW scheme has accordingly been defined as the ratio of net area irrigated to net irrigable area expressed as percentage. Since the two types of utilisation rates are estimated by using two different methods, the rates may show a little difference. However, for a rough comparison the utilisation rates for different schemes and location under government and private sector are shown in Table 5.1.

Table 5.1 shows that utilisation rate under government sector irrigation schemes is very low (34.24%). There is also widespread variation in utilisation rates among various schemes. While the lowest utilisation rate is observed under Sessa LIS (18.28%), the highest utilisation rate is found under Jamuna Irrigation Scheme (66.92%). Barring Jamuna none of

Table 5.1 : Utilisation Rates of Different Schemes

(In percentage)

Government Sector		*Private Sector*	
Scheme	*Utilisation Rate*	*Location*	*Utilisation Rate*
(1)	*(2)*	*(3)*	*(4)*
Sessa	18.28	Dihing Thekerani	45.32
Duliabam	39.29	Panigaon Kalakhowa	41.52
Mandia	30.5	Dibrugarh District	43.42
Puthimari	41.25	Katimari Grant	40.04
Chenga	42.5	Gotonga	40.73
Kaldiya	19.35	Nagaon District	40.40
Jamuna	66.92	Keotkuchi	68.20
		Domoni	62.65
		Barpeta District	66.06
Overall	34.24*	Overall	51.92

* Calculated by taking weighted average.

the sample irrigation schemes has utilisation rate above 50 per cent. This depicts a case of clear underutilisation of irrigation potential created.

Compared to government irrigation schemes, utilisation rate under privately owned shallow tube wells (STWs) is found to be higher (51.92). There is, however, variation in this utilisation rate across locations of the schemes. The highest utilisation rate is observed in Barpeta district followed by Dibrugarh and Nagaon in that order. Keotkuchi in Barpeta district has achieved the highest utilisation rate while the lowest rate is observed in Katimari Grant in Nagaon District. Even the utilisation rate of private shallow tube wells can do with considerable improvement.

As mentioned above due to difference in the methodology of computation of the utilisation rates for government and private irrigation projects, the rates for the two categories are not strictly comparable. Moreover, a standard measure such as the one used for the government owned projects may give a somewhat misleading indication of water utilisation in the context of Assam as demand for irrigation in the *kharif* season is limited in most parts of this flood-prone and monsoon-heavy state. To illustrate this point, the two extreme examples of the Jamuna and the Mandia projects may be considered. The Jamuna project caters to a rain-shadow area where monsoon precipitation is low compared to the other parts of the state. Thus irrigation is needed and used not only for the non-*kharif* but also for the *kharif* crops. Accordingly, gross area irrigated of the project is comparatively higher giving a higher value of the utilisation rate. In contrast, the Mandia project caters to a chronically flood affected area and due to certainty and regularity of floods in monsoon season, farmers there cannot raise the *kharif* crop. Hence the crop in the dry season is extremely important for the farmers for which irrigation is also essential. It was observed in the field study that farmers take active interest in keeping the irrigation water flowing in the dry season and utilisation of irrigation water as well as use of productivity raising practices in that season is impressive. But since irrigation cannot be and is not utilised during the *kharif* season, the gross irrigated area for this project does not come out high. This depresses the utilisation rate for this project. But in view of the just mentioned facts, the utilisation rate does not reflect the efficiency of utilisation in this project.

The insights gathered in the field study indicate that the utilisation rate under private STW schemes is constrained by the following factors —

(i) The full capacity of some of the STWs could not be exploited because of fragmentation of holdings. Due to non-availability of a minimum size of compact land, fullest utilisation of the STWs is not taking place.

(ii) Some of the pumps used for irrigation in the field are found to be very old. Because of depreciation over the years, these pumps are not in a position to deliver water at the rate of estimated potential. Thus the assumption of 2 (two) hectares of net command area for each of these old STWs is an exaggeration in so far as capacity of the old STWs is concerned.

5.2 Use of Irrigation Water

The discussion under the head 'utilisation rate' gives a picture of utilisation of irrigation water under different schemes. But as already mentioned the two pictures are not strictly speaking comparable. Therefore, the question of utilisation of irrigation water under different schemes has also been examined from a different angle using the data collected in the field study for different irrigation schemes. For this purpose, we would like to start by looking at use of irrigation water by sample farmers under different forms.

The use of irrigation water under different schemes is shown in Tables 5.2 and 5.3.

Table 5.2 : Percentage of Irrigated Land in Combined Gross Cropped Area of Sample Farms under Government Schemes

Name of the scheme	*Percentage*
(1)	*(2)*
Sessa	23.46
Duliabam	44.98
Mandia	74.33
Puthimari	49.51
Chenga	62.37
Kaldiya	49.20
Jamuna	74.24
Overall	58.25

The table 5.2 show that irrigation coverage under the government schemes is about 58 per cent of the gross cropped area. The figure for private shallow tube-wells is marginally higher at 58.86 per cent. Thus, there is still about 41 per cent of the gross cropped area which does not use irrigation water for raising crops.

Table 5.3 : Percentage of Irrigated Land in Combined Gross Cropped Area of Sample Farms under Private Schemes

Name of the Scheme	*Percentage*
(1)	*(2)*
Dihing Thekerani	50.23
Panigaon Kalakhowa	48.23
Katimari Grant	49.59
Gotonga	54.70
Keotkuchi	75.53
Domoni	64.66
Overall	58.86

5.3 Aailability of Irrigation Water as per Farmers' Requirements

Though the utilisation rate has been found to be better for private schemes than government schemes, the rate is relatively less under all types of schemes. On the other hand, as shown in the preceding section, about 58 per cent of total cropped area of farmers under both government and private schemes is irrigated. The question which arises is whether low utilisation rate is due to insufficient demand or failures in supply management. In this context, it may be worthwhile to examine farmers' responses to the query whether they receive irrigation water in right time and in required quantity. So, an attempt has been made in the following section to examine the availability of water in the field as per farmers' requirement.

While examining the availability of irrigation water in the field it is noticed that the amount varies from household to household in the command areas of the schemes themselves. The variation is noticed not only across farms in a scheme but also across different schemes. While the smaller schemes show some kind of homogeneity regarding availability of water, major and medium irrigation schemes exhibit sharp variations across farm households in different reaches in the command area of the schemes. Availability of irrigation water in different government irrigation schemes is presented in Table 5.4.

Table 5.4 : Percentage of Sample Farmers Receiving Irrigation Water as per Requirement (Government Schemes)

Sl. No.	*Schemes*	*Percentage of Farmers*
(1)	*(2)*	*(3)*
1	Sessa	41.67
2	Duliabam	60.00
3	Mandia	91.67
4	Puthimari	60.00
5	Chenga	50.00
6	Kaldiya	45.00
7	Jamuna	70.97
	Total	60.95

Table 5.4 shows that of a total of 105 farm households, about 60.95 per cent have received water as per their requirements. This relatively high percentage, however, is due only to a better performance of Mandia and Jamuna Irrigation schemes which have been able to supply water to the field as per requirements of 91.67 per cent and 70.97 per cent respectively of the sample farmers in the command areas of the schemes. Barring these two, the other schemes could supply water to the fields as per requirements of about 40 to 60 per cent of the sample farmers only. Schemewise, Sessa has the worst performance in so far as satisfying the requirements of the sample farmers in the form of supplying water to the field is concerned. It could provide water to the field as per requirement of only 41.67 per cent of the sample farmers. Kaldiya, which is a medium scheme, could satisfy the needs of 45 per cent of the sample farmers in the command area. The main problems associated with these two schemes are the problem with canal structure, non-

availability of water in the canal at the time of requirement and erratic supply of electricity. Mandia irrigation scheme could provide water to about 91.67 per cent of farmers as per their requirements. The better performance of this scheme can be attributed to the good functioning of *Pathar Parichalana Samiti* (Field Management Committee) of the area which is looking after the minor repairing works of the scheme themselves in the absence of fund of the government for maintaining irrigation schemes.

Although the overall performance of the Jamuna Irrigation scheme is good, there is a marked variation in the performance of the scheme in different reaches. For example, while the scheme could provide water to 100 per cent of the sample farmers in the head reach as per requirement, the corresponding figure for the tail reach is only 30 per cent. The middle reach of the scheme could supply water to 80 per cent of the sample farmers as per their requirements. The problems for low availability of irrigation water in the tail reach arise because of a number of factors. These include non-availability of water in the canal, non-release of water at the time of requirement, broken canal, inhabitation in the command area, theft of materials of the canal etc. Table 5.5 shows availability of irrigation water in the field under private schemes.

Table 5.5 : Percentage of Sample Farmers Receiving Irrigation Water as per Requirement (Private Schemes)

Sl. No.	*Schemes*	*Percentage of Farmers*
(1)	*(2)*	*(3)*
1	Dihing Thekerani	81.82
2	Panigaon Kalakhowa	90.91
3	Dibrugarh District	86.36
4	Katimari Grant	75.00
5	Gotonga	66.67
6	Nagaon District	70.83
7	Keotkuchi	100.00
8	Domoni	80.00
9	Barpeta District	90.48
10	Overall	82.09

Compared to government irrigation schemes, privately owned shallow tube wells seem to have a better performance in so far as providing water to the fields as per requirements is concerned. As against 60.95 per cent under government sector, proportion of sample farmers getting water as per requirements under shallow tube wells is much higher at 82.09 per cent. This is mainly because of better maintenance of the small-scale irrigation schemes under private sector compared to the government schemes. Only in case of 17.91 per cent of sample farmers, it is found that availability of irrigation water in the field was not as per requirement. However, it is observed that in all the cases where irrigation availability was not as per requirement, the pump sets were either shared or hired, not owned. Water could not be made available to the field in time because the pumps were not available at the time of requirement. Thus, it was found that there is a direct relationship between timely availability of irrigation water in the field and owning an irrigation system. Districtwise, Barpeta could provide water to the fields of 90.48 per cent of sample farmers in the two villages of Keotkuchi and Domoni as per their requirements. It was closely followed by Dibrugarh which could provide timely irrigation water to 86.36 per cent of sample farmers while Nagaon could satisfy the needs of 70.83 per cent of sample farmers so far as timely and adequate supply of irrigation water is concerned. Thus, it has been observed that the performance of privately owned shallow tube wells is better than government irrigation in supplying water to the fields according to the needs of the beneficiary farmers.

5.4 Reasons Cited for Non-availibility of Irrigation Water in Time and in Adequate Quantity

The schedule used for collecting data from farm households in the fieldwork also included a query about the reason for non-availability of water in the command areas of the schemes at the time of requirement. On the basis of the farmers' responses, the following factors have been identified as responsible for low utilisation of irrigation capacity :

5.4.1 Surface Flow Schemes (Government)

1. Poor canal system causing unequal distribution of water. For the farmers in the tail reach water in adequate quantity and in right time is not available.
2. Water is not released in time and therefore farmers, particularly in the middle and lower reaches, do not get timely water. Upper reach people resist in releasing water in time.
3. Some portions of the canals are broken and require repairing. But the government has not been able to do so in the absence of adequate fund for maintenance.
4. In some of the flow schemes water from the canal leaks because of a number of outlets. The gates of these outlets are either broken or stolen. The low-lying areas under the schemes are waterlogged because of excess water flowing through these outlets in summer.
5. Inhabitation of people has taken place in certain parts of the command area of the lower reach in Jamuna Irrigation Scheme thereby damaging the canal structure. The farmers in these areas do not get sufficient water at the time of requirement.
6. A portion of the command area in the lower reach of Jamuna scheme suffers from the problem of flood in summer due to the nearby Dimoru river. The farmers in this portion of the command area of the scheme do not get water from the scheme because of flood.
7. In a few schemes, cattle created problems in the form of damaging the brick canal system.
8. Theft of materials like gates etc. is also not

uncommon. This is partly responsible for water-logging in low-lying areas under the scheme.

5.4.2 *Lift Schemes (Government)*

Most of the lift irrigation schemes suffer due to mechanical problems of the pumps, supply of electricity and distribution of water to the fields, etc. Each of these tasks is performed by a separate Department of the State Government and there is hardly any coordination among these Departments. On the whole the problems of the lift irrigation schemes can be summarised as follows—

1. Supply of irrigation water is not regular due to erratic supply of electricity.
2. In some of the schemes because of minor mechanical problems pumps are not operating to the maximum capacity. Many of the pumps are inoperational which resulted in underutilisation of irrigation capacity of the schemes.
3. In the case of distribution also, because of broken canal structure, farmers are not getting adequate water in the field. Broken canal leads to excess water in the low-lying areas. Repairing of the canals is required.
4. In some schemes a portion of the canals is found to be earthen. This results in loss of water in conveyance.
5. In some cases canal lining was found to be defective. In the absence of adequate land reform measures like levelling of land, etc. portions of the command area are deprived of irrigation water.

5.4.3 *Ground Water Lift Schemes (Private)*

Though the observed rates of utilisation of the private shallow tube wells are better, the rates are by no means nearly full. The fuller utilisation of irrigation potential created under these STWs has been found to be restrained mainly by the following :

1. For farmers using irrigation by hiring pump sets, non-availability of the pump at the time of requirement is found to be one major problem affecting timely supply of water.
2. A minimum size of 2 hectares of the plot of land is required for effective operation of the shallow tube wells. But it was often found that due to fragmentation most of the farmers possessing STWs did not have the compact minimum area of land required for maximum utilisation of the potential created. As a result, fullest utilisation of the created potential of STWs has not been possible.

5.5 Cropwise Irrigation

The sample farmers under different irrigation schemes have differences not only in the use of irrigation water but also in use of irrigation for different crops. The cropwise irrigation under different irrigation schemes is shown in Table 5.6 and 5.7.

Table 5.6 shows that there is no definite pattern regarding use of irrigation water for different crops. For all the schemes as a whole, HYV winter paddy accounted for the highest amount of irrigation water (35.01%). This is followed by traditional winter paddy (15.86%). Thus winter paddy as a whole accounted for about 50.87 per cent of the total area under irrigation. Schemewise, Sessa and Puthimari had their maximum irrigated area under vegetables, while Mandia and Chenga had their highest irrigated area under HYV summer paddy. In Duliabam and Jamuna irrigation schemes HYV winter paddy had the maximum area under irrigation whereas in Kaldiya traditional winter paddy is grown under

Table 5.6 : Cropwise Distribution of Gross Area Irrigated (Government Schemes)

(In percentages)

Crops / *Schemes*	*Winter Paddy*		*Autumn Paddy*		*Summer Paddy*		*Rape & Mustard*	*Wheat*	*Vege-tables*	*Total*
	Tradi-tional	*HYV*	*Tradi-tional*	*HYV*	*Tradi-tional*	*HYV*				
(1)	*(2)*	*(3)*	*(4)*	*(5)*	*(6)*	*(7)*	*(8)*	*(9)*	*(10)*	*(11)*
Sessa	3.51	5.26	5.26	33.33	0.00	0.00	0.00	0.00	52.63	100.00
Mandia	0.00	0.00	0.00	0.00	0.00	82.96	15.56	0.00	1.48	100.00
Duliabam	28.16	33.01	0.00	31.07	0.00	0.00	0.00	0.00	7.77	100.00
Puthimari	0.00	4.76	25.40	12.70	0.00	0.00	0.00	4.76	52.38	100.00
Chenga	1.97	34.43	0.00	0.00	0.00	41.64	3.28	0.00	18.69	100.00
Kaldiya	44.52	24.75	23.59	0.33	0.00	0.00	1.33	2.33	3.16	100.00
Jamuna	12.32	55.81	0.00	26.10	0.00	0.00	0.00	0.00	5.77	100.00
Overall	15.86	35.01	7.20	15.04	0.00	11.92	2.04	0.88	12.05	100.00

maximum area with irrigation. The relatively higher proportion of winter paddy in gross irrigated area under Jamuna scheme may be attributed to the fact that the scheme is located in a rain shadow area. So the demand for irrigation in the area is not only for dry season crops, but also for *kharif* crops, i.e. winter paddy. Irrigation has not been able to induce the farmers much to switch over to non-winter paddy crops under these irrigation schemes. However, under Sessa, Duliabam and Jamuna irrigation schemes considerable amount of irrigated land was under HYV autumn rice which shows some degree of crop diversification.

Table 5.7 shows that in case of private schemes irrigation is utilised to a greater extent for non-rice crops in general and non-winter paddy crops in particular than under government schemes. This indicates that private irrigation may have facilitated the crop diversification more than government irrigation schemes. Vegetables have predominated irrigated land in all the schemes except in Katimari grant in Nagaon and Keotkuchi in Barpeta district. It is observed that in Katimari Grant and Gotonga, HYV summer paddy had assumed much significance with the availability of irrigation water in the field. In Keotkuchi in

Table 5.7 : Cropwise Distribution of Gross Area Irrigated (Private Schemes)

(In percentages)

Crops / *Locations*	*Winter Paddy*		*Autumn Paddy*		*Summer Paddy*		*Rape & Mustard*	*Wheat*	*Vege-tables*	*Total*
	Tradi-tional	*HYV*	*Tradi-tional*	*HYV*	*Tradi-tional*	*HYV*				
(1)	*(2)*	*(3)*	*(4)*	*(5)*	*(6)*	*(7)*	*(8)*	*(9)*	*(10)*	*(11)*
Katimari Grant	0.00	0.00	0.00	0.00	0.00	84.78	0.00	0.00	15.22	100.00
Gotonga	0.00	0.63	0.00	0.63	0.00	38.13	4.38	0.00	56.25	100.00
Dihing Thekerani	0.00	0.00	26.53	3.71	0.00	0.00	0.00	0.00	69.76	100.00
Panigaon Kalakhowa	0.00	1.84	9.19	29.78	0.00	0.00	4.78	0.00	54.41	100.00
Keotkuchi	1.12	12.85	6.33	22.91	0.00	0.93	22.34	4.84	28.68	100.00
Domoni	0.00	0.00	0.00	0.00	0.00	12.96	0.00	09.97	77.08	100.00
Overall	0.36	4.45	7.75	12.77	0.00	13.51	8.31	3.33	49.52	100.00

Barpeta district availability of irrigation water had made possible growing of all major crops with some greater emphasis on crops like vegetables, HYV autumn paddy and rape and mustard. For all the schemes taken together, vegetables are grown in maximum amount of area followed by HYV summer paddy and HYV autumn paddy. Thus diversification of crops in terms of non-paddy crops in total crops and non-winter paddy crops in total crops has taken place under the schemes under investigation.

5.6 Cropping Pattern and Cropping Intensity

The cultivated area, cropping pattern and cropping intensity of the sample farmers in the seven government schemes are shown in Table 5.8.

The figures in Table 5.8 show that about 77 per cent of the combined total cropped area of the 105 sample farmers under government schemes is under rice. In Duliabam and Jamuna schemes about 89 and 85 per cent respectively of total cropped area are under rice. In Sessa percentage of area under rice is about 56 per cent of the total cropped area under

Table 5.8 : Area under Different Crops, their Percentage Shares in Gross Cropped Area and Cropping Intensity under Sample Government Schemes

Crops \ Schemes	Area (in hectares)							Total
	Sessa	Duliabam	Mandia	Puthimari	Chenga	Kaldiya	Jamuna	
(1)	(2)	(3)	(4)	(5)	(6)	(7)	(8)	(9)
Autumn Paddy	4.22 (12.31)	2.54 (16.57)	0 (0.00)	6.69 (19.64)	0 (0.00)	15.26 (19.27)	24.03 (20.14)	52.74 (15.67)
Winter Paddy	14.99 (43.74)	11.11 (72.47)	0 (0.00)	17.74 (52.07)	16.80 (51.33)	45.92 (57.99)	76.77 (64.36)	183.20 (54.51)
Summer Paddy	0 (0.00)	0 (0.00)	15.80 (73.08)	0 (0.00)	8.10 (24.75)	0 (0.00)	0 (0.00)	23.90 (7.10)
Total Paddy	19.21 (56.05)	13.65 (89.04)	15.80 (73.08)	24.43 (71.71)	24.90 (76.08)	61.18 (77.27)	100.80 (84.50)	259.84 (77.22)
Rape & Mustard	1.07 (3.12)	0 (0.00)	4.75 (21.97)	0 (0.00)	1.87 (5.71)	2.07 (2.61)	0 (0.00)	9.77 (2.90)
Pulses	0.67 (1.96)	0 (0.00)	0 (0.00)	0 (0.00)	0.07 (0.21)	1.74 (2.20)	0 (0.00)	2.48 (0.74)
Others	0.47 (1.37)	0 (0.00)	0 (0.00)	0.80 (2.35)	0.13 (0.40)	0.94 (1.19)	2.5 (2.10)	4.84 (1.44)
Vegetables	12.85 (37.50)	1.67 (10.89)	1.07 (4.95)	8.84 (25.95)	5.49 (16.77)	13.25 (16.73)	15.98 (13.40)	59.16 (17.58)
Gross Cropped Area	34.27 (100.00)	15.33 (100.00)	21.62 (100)	34.07 (100.00)	32.73 (100)	79.18 (100)	119.29 (100.00)	336.49 (100.00)
Net Sown Area	20.42	10.84	16.53	17.74	20.55	47.32	78.38	211.78
Cropping intensity (in percentage)	162.62	141.36	130.77	192.08	159.28	167.33	152.19	158.89

Note : Figures in parentheses represent percentages of gross cropped area.

the scheme. The cropping intensity under all these schemes is found to be 158.89 per cent with the lowest cropping intensity at Mandia (130.77%) and highest at Puthimari (192.83%). The low cropping intensity in Mandia Irrigation Scheme is due to the fact that the command area of the scheme is a flood prone area and as such practice of multiple cropping is not widespread. In Puthimari where the cropping intensity is the highest, the share of paddy to total cropped area is also somewhat lower. But in Mandia where cropping intensity was the lowest, the share of paddy to the total cropped area is not the highest, although it is at somewhat a higher level. The share of paddy was the highest under the Duliabam Irrigation Scheme (89%). The relatively lower share of paddy in the gross cropped area is indicative of the fact that in all the schemes under investigation, some kind of crop diversification has taken place. Apart from paddy, the other notable crops raised by the farmers under these schemes are vegetables, rape and mustard and pulses. Area under different crops, their percentage share in the GCA and cropping intensity in the sample farms under STWs are presented in Table 5.9.

Table 5.9 : Area under Different Crops, their Percentage Shares in Gross Cropped Area and Cropping Intensity in Different Sample Locations with Private Irrigation

Schemes / *Crops*	*Area in hectares*						
	Dihing Thekerani	*Panigaon Kalakhowa*	*Katimari Grant*	*Gotonga*	*Keotkuchi*	*Domoni*	*Total*
(1)	*(2)*	*(3)*	*(4)*	*(5)*	*(6)*	*(7)*	*(8)*
Autumn paddy	11.11 (15.47)	24.63 (32.62)	0 (0.00)	1.74 (4.44)	22.36 (23.49)	5.35 (8.58)	65.19 (17.02)
Winter paddy	28.51 (39.70)	26.64 (35.28)	16.67 (42.73)	13.32 (34.01)	27.18 (28.56)	9.24 (14.83)	121.55 (31.74)
Summer paddy	0 (0.00)	0 (0.00)	16.40 (42.04)	7.97 (20.35)	0.67 (0.70)	5.22 (8.38)	30.25 (7.90)
Total Paddy	39.63 (55.18)	51.27 (67.90)	33.07 (84.77)	23.03 (58.81)	50.20 (52.74)	19.81 (31.79)	217.00 (56.66)
Rape & mustard	1.34 (1.87)	3.75 (4.97)	0 (0.00)	0.94 (2.40)	19.55 (20.54)	0 (0.00)	25.57 (6.68)
Pulses	1.00 (1.39)	0.67 (0.89)	0 (0.00)	0 (0.00)	0.27 (0.28)	3.95 (6.34)	5.89 (1.54)
Others	0 (0.00)	0 (0.00)	1.47 (3.77)	2.48 (6.33)	4.55 (4.78)	4.69 (7.53)	13.19 (3.44)
Vegetables	29.85 (41.56)	19.81 (26.24)	4.47 (11.46)	12.72 (32.48)	20.62 (21.66)	33.87 (54.35)	121.34 (31.68)
Gross Cropped Area	71.82 (100)	75.50 (100)	39.01 (100)	39.16 (100)	95.18 (100)	62.32 (100)	382.99 (100)
Net Sown area	41.23	36.55	17.74	17.74	48.73	32.73	194.71
Cropping Intensity (in percentage)	174.19	206.59	219.92	220.75	195.33	190.39	196.69

Note : Figures in parentheses represent percentages to gross cropped area.

Percentage of non-paddy crops in GCA is found to be more in privately owned shallow tube wells than in government schemes. It is evident from Table 5.9 that rice is grown in only about 57 per cent of the total cropped area of 382.99 hectares under all schemes. The corresponding figure for government schemes is about 77 per cent. Schemewise, Domoni in Barpeta district has the lowest percentage of area under rice, while Katimari Grant in Nagaon district has the highest percentage of area under rice. While the figure for the former is as low as 31.79 per cent, the figure for the latter is placed at a much higher level at 84.77 per cent. This is due to the fact that Domoni is predominantly a vegetable growing area while Katimari Grant is a low-lying area suitable mainly for rice only. Area under rice as percentage to the total cropped area for other schemes lies between 50 to 70. Apart from rice, vegetables and rape and mustard are the two important crops raised in the areas under study. Pulses, wheat and jute are also grown in the areas, although in lesser areas. The cropping intensity is the highest in Gotonga in Nagaon district and lowest in Dihing Thekerani in Dibrugarh district. The cropping intensity for all the areas under STWs is 196.69 per cent which is much higher than the corresponding figure for government schemes (158.39%).

Irrigation is also found to help in changing the cropping pattern of the region concerned. This change which we call crop diversification can be examined under two heads (i) change in the share of non-paddy crops in GCA and (ii) change in the share of non-winter paddy crops in GCA. An attempt has been made here to examine the extent to which diversification of crops has taken place as a result of availability of irrigation in the study area. The results are presented in Table 5.10.

Table 5.10 shows that farmers under privately owned schemes have been able to achieve greater crop diversification compared to farmers under government

Table 5.10 : Extent of Crop Diversification across Schemes and Districts

District / Schemes	Dibrugarh		Nagaon		Barpeta		Overall	
	% of non-paddy crops in GCA	*% of non-winter paddy in GCA*	*% of non-paddy crops in GCA*	*% of non-winter paddy in GCA*	*% of non-paddy crops in GCA*	*% of non-winter paddy in GCA*	*% of non-paddy crops in GCA*	*% of non-winter paddy in GCA*
(1)	*(2)*	*(3)*	*(4)*	*(5)*	*(6)*	*(7)*	*(8)*	*(9)*
Government	33.73	20.57	15.50	23.84	24.47	36.30	22.44	45.32
Private	38.30	39.32	28.25	46.54	55.56	47.99	43.34	68.26

owned and managed schemes. Share of non-paddy crops as percentage of GCA for government schemes is found to be the highest in Nagaon district and lowest in Barpeta district. Similarly, for private schemes, this ratio is the highest in Barpeta district and the lowest in Nagaon district. Share of non-winter paddy crops in total cropped area is the highest in Barpeta district for both government and private schemes followed by Dibrugarh and Nagaon in that order. The overall share of non-paddy crops to GCA is 22.44 per cent for government and 43.34 per cent for private schemes. Again, the share of non-winter paddy crops to GCA for all the districts taken together is 45.32 per cent for government schemes and 68.26 per cent for private schemes. All these have established the fact that winter paddy has remained the most dominant crop in total paddy area even after introduction of irrigation. However, share of non-paddy crops in the gross cropped area has been gradually increasing under both government and private schemes for all the districts.

5.7 Use of High Yielding Varieties

The extent of use of HYVs by sample farmers under government schemes is presented in Table 5.11.

Use of HYVs by sample farmers under government

Table 5.11 : Percentage of Area under HYV in Combined Rice Acerage of Sample Farms under Government Schemes

Schemes	Percentage of HYV Area			
	Sali (Winter) Rice	*Ahu (Autumn) Rice*	*Boro (Summer) Rice*	*Total Rice*
(1)	*(2)*	*(3)*	*(4)*	*(5)*
Sessa	45.98	46.03	–	45.99
Duliabam	33.73	100.00	–	46.08
Mandia	–	–	100.00	100.00
Puthimari	25.09	32.00	–	26.98
Chenga	53.04	–	100.00	68.48
Kaldiya	45.77	11.40	–	37.20
Jamuna	65.30	100.00	–	73.57
Total	51.88	61.42	100.00	58.24

schemes was almost universal in the sense that out of 105 sample farmers 99 (about 94 per cent) have adopted high yielding paddy varieties in the seven schemes under study. The varieties which are found to be popular among sample farmers are Mahsuri, Pankaj, Bahadur, Ranjit, Chilarai, Jaya, Jyoti-Bishnu, etc. But interestingly, the spread of area under high yielding varieties has been found to have remained fairly limited. The highest percentage of 100 per cent HYV area is recorded in Mandia scheme. This scheme is a fairly successful one running mainly with the co-operation of the beneficiary farmers. The area being a low-lying and flood affected one, people have to raise a single crop only in the entire season. This prompts people to use high yielding varieties to have higher productivity of crops. In terms of area under HYV paddy, Mandia is followed by Jamuna and Chenga schemes which have about 74 and 68 per cent of total paddy area under HYVs respectively. In Puthimari, percentage of area under HYVs is the lowest at 26.98 per cent. The command area of this scheme is basically a vegetable growing one and as such more attention is given to production of vegetables than on paddy. The proportion of HYV area in total rice acreage of sample farmers under government schemes is found to be about 58 per cent.

Table 5.12 shows the percentage of areas under HYV paddy for private schemes.

Table 5.12 : Percentage of Area under HYV in Combined Rice Acerage of Sample Farms under Private Schemes

Schemes	*Percentage of HYV Area*			
	Sali (Winter) Rice	*Ahu (Autumn) Rice*	*Boro (Summer) Rice*	*Total Rice*
(1)	*(2)*	*(3)*	*(4)*	*(5)*
Dihing Thekerani	20.78	3.89	0.00	24.66
Panigaon Kalakhowa	27.42	23.76	0.00	51.17
Katimari	38.96	0.00	100.00	69.23
Gotonga	53.77	7.69	100.00	66.28
Keotkuchi	52.22	73.65	100.00	62.40
Domoni	0.00	0.00	100.00	26.35
Overall	41.24	46.51	100.00	51.02

In case of private shallow tube well schemes, percentage of HYV area in total paddy acerage is about 51 per cent which is slightly lower than the figure in case of government schemes. The relatively lesser proportion of area under HYV rice in private sector can be attributed to the lower HYV rice acerage in the two locations of Dibrugarh district. In these two locations, the practice of cultivation of summer rice is not noticed. Additionally, the area under HYV rice in case of winter and autumn rice is fairly limited. Again, out of a total of 67 farm households under STW, 61 (about 91 per cent) have been adopting HYVs. The corresponding figure for government irrigation schemes is 94 per cent. Thus there is very little to distinguish between government irrigation schemes and privately owned STWs in so far as adoption of HYVs is concerned. The highest percentage of HYV area under total paddy is observed in Katimari Grant in Nagaon district (69%). This is closely followed by Gotonga in Nagaon district and Keotkuchi in Barpeta district. The lowest percentage of HYV area under total paddy is found at Dihing Thekerani in Dibrugarh district (24.66%) which is closely followed by Domoni in Barpeta district (26.35%). The farmers in Dihing Thekerani in Dibrugarh district are new to the adoption of HYVs particularly in case of paddy although they have started growing HYV vegetables after installation of private shallow tube wells after 1996.

5.8 Use of Soil Nutrients

As in the case of use of HYVs, the use of chemical fertilizers was almost universal among the sample farmers. The use of chemical fertilizers by sample farmers during the reference year in different schemes is shown in Table 5.13.

Table 5.13 : Districtwise Chemical Fertilizer (N+P+K) Consumption (kg/hect.) by Sample Farmers

District	*Government Schemes*	*Private Schemes*	*Overall*
(1)	*(2)*	*(3)*	*(4)*
Dibrugarh	79.85	37.35	47.77
Nagaon	125.81	71.78	104.18
Barpeta	51.02	180.76	113.94
Overall	81.54	103.35	93.22

Table 5.13 reveals that the consumption of fertilizer in the sample farms is very high. The overall fertilizer consumption rate of 93.22 kg per hectare is found to be more than six times the figure of fertilizer consumption rate for the state for the year 1996-97 (as given in Table 3.4 of chapter 3). This rate of fertilizer consumption in the sample farms compares favourably with the rate of consumption of fertilizer in agriculturally advanced states like U.P., Tamil Nadu, etc. The higher fertilizer consumption in the sample area is to be expected as the sample includes only irrigated farms. There are instances of using overdoses of fertilizer in the sample farms. In some cases, the amount of fertilizer applied in the field was found to be even more than five times the amount prescribed by the Department of Agriculture of Government of Assam.

With availability of irrigation farmers in Assam also tend

to use productivity raising inputs in abundance. Table 5.13 also shows that on the average, farmers operating under private irrigation system tend to use fertilizer at a higher dose than those operating under government irrigation.

5.9 Yield of Rice

Yield of crops is an important parameter of measuring the effectiveness of irrigation schemes. To have comparative discussion of yield under different types of irrigation schemes we have estimated yield of the principal crop grown i.e. rice for the sample farms. The results for the two types of irrigation schemes are presented in Tables 5.14 and 5.15.

Table 5.14 : Seasonwise Schemewise Yield of Rice under Government Schemes (quintal/hectare)

Crops / *Schemes*	*Autumn Rice*		*Winter Rice*		*Summer Rice*		*Total*		*Overall Yield*
	Traditional	*HYV*	*Traditional*	*HYV*	*Traditional*	*HYV*	*Traditional*	*HYV*	
(1)	*(2)*	*(3)*	*(4)*	*(5)*	*(6)*	*(7)*	*(8)*	*(9)*	*(10)*
Sessa	17.23	19.84	19.33	25.34	–	–	18.87	24.13	21.29
Duliabam	–	20.89	20.20	23.72	–	–	20.20	24.68	22.16
Mandia	–	–	–	–	–	44.47	–	44.47	44.47
Puthimari	13.86	17.01	15.03	21.22	–	–	14.74	19.86	16.12
Chenga	–	–	18.72	29.59	–	30.64	18.72	30.09	26.51
Kaldiya	13.52	17.06	19.90	25.85	–	–	18.35	25.18	20.89
Jamuna	–	30.65	20.67	33.29	–	–	20.67	32.44	29.33
Overall	15.32	27.61	19.26	29.78	–	39.78	18.52	30.89	25.73

It is evident from Table 5.14 that the overall yield of rice under different government schemes is very high (25.73 qtl/ha). This is much higher than the average yield of rice for the state as a whole at 14.80 quintal per hectare in 1999-2000 (CMIE, 2001). In fact, this figure can be compared with the average yield of rice of the agriculturally developed states like Haryana, Andhra Pradesh, Karnataka, etc. There is a sharp difference in the yield of rice between traditional and High Yielding Varieties. For example, the yield of traditional varieties of autumn rice is 15.32 quintal per hectare whereas for HYV it is 27.61 quintal per hectare. Similarly, for winter rice, the yield of traditional variety is 19.26 and for HYVs it is 29.78. The figures for yield of total rice for traditional and HYVs are 18.52 and 30.89 quintals per hectare respectively. There is variation in yields between alternative forms of rice as well. While the yield of HYV autumn rice is 27.61 quintals per hectare, the figure for HYV summer rice is 39.78 quintals per hectare. Schemewise, the highest yield is observed in Jamuna Irrigation Scheme both for autumn and winter rice whereas for summer rice the maximum yield is found in Mandia Irrigation Scheme. In fact, the yield of summer rice observed under this scheme is the highest among all forms of rice and also among all the government schemes.

Table 5.15 : Seasonwise Locationwise Yield of Rice under Private Schemes

(quintalhectare)

Crops / *Schemes*	*Autumn Rice*		*Winter Rice*		*Summer Rice*		*Total*		*Overall Yield*
	Traditional	*HYV*	*Traditional*	*HYV*	*Traditional*	*HYV*	*Traditional*	*HYV*	
(1)	*(2)*	*(3)*	*(4)*	*(5)*	*(6)*	*(7)*	*(8)*	*(9)*	*(10)*
Dihing Thekerani	24.67	24.71	22.23	29.40	–	–	23.01	28.66	24.41
Panigaon Kalakhowa	13.17	27.86	16.38	30.48	–	–	14.79	29.27	22.20
Dibrugarh District	18.17	27.51	19.99	30.08	–	–	19.26	29.10	23.16
Katimari Grant	–	–	21.80	26.35	–	40.46	21.80	36.46	31.95
Gotonga	11.84	8.67	19.42	26.17	–	27.59	17.85	26.76	23.76
Nagaon District	11.84	8.67	20.90	26.26	–	36.25	20.09	32.58	28.58
Keotkuchi	21.03	43.85	19.10	29.61	–	37.35	19.70	37.26	30.66
Domoni	15.29	–	21.42	–	–	37.54	19.17	37.54	24.01
Barpeta District	18.30	43.85	20.06	29.61	–	37.52	19.47	37.30	28.78
Total	17.92	36.30	20.22	28.91	–	36.50	19.47	33.01	26.37

Table 5.15 shows that the overall yield of rice for private

shallow tube wells is 26.37 qtl. per hectare which is slightly higher than the corresponding figure for government schemes (25.73 qtl./hectare). While the yield for traditional variety is 19.47 qtl. per hectare, the same for HYVs is 33.01 qtl. per hectare. Cropwise, the highest yield is achieved for HYV summer rice followed by HYV winter rice and HYV autumn rice in that order. Thus in both government and private irrigation schemes, the yield of summer rice is higher than autumn and winter rice which naturally calls for expansion of area under this crop. The variation in the yields of traditional and HYVs is more pronounced in case of private schemes compared to government irrigation schemes. Districtwise, Barpeta has the highest overall yield followed closely by Nagaon and Dibrugarh in that order. In Keotkuchi under Barpeta district, the highest yield for autumn rice is observed (43.85). This is the highest yield of autumn rice for both private schemes and government irrigation schemes taken together.

5.10 Extent of Contact of Sample Farmers with Extension Agencies

Extension work has been an important factor in diffusion of improved practices among farmers. Therefore in the schedule used for field study, questions were included to record the influence of government extension agencies on the farming practices of the sample farmers. The farmers' responses to these queries have been codified and scores awarded. On the basis of the scores, the level of contact with extension agencies have been categorised into (i) very good, (ii) good, (iii) moderate, and (iv) poor. (The details of codification process and the score system is reported in Appendix 5.A to this chapter).

The distribution of sample farmers according to the level of contact with extension agencies is shown in Tables 5.16 and 5.17.

Table 5.16 : Distribution of Sample Farmers under Different Government Irrigation Schemes according to the Level of Contact with Extension Agencies

Schemes / Level of Contact	Sessa	Duliabam	Mandia	Puthimari	Chenga	Kaldiya	Jamuna	Total
(1)	(2)	(3)	(4)	(5)	(6)	(7)	(8)	(9)
Very good	0	0	0	0	0	1	0	1 (0.95)
Good	3	9	1	3	5	7	8	36 (34.29)
Moderate	4	1	7	5	5	7	12	41 (39.05)
Poor	5	0	4	2	0	5	11	27 (25.71)
Total	12	10	12	10	10	20	31	105 (100.00)

Note : Figures in parentheses represent percentages of total sample.

Table 5.16 shows that only about 35 per cent of the sample farmers had good or very good contact with the extension agencies and were also benefited from the service. About 26 per cent of the total sample farmers under government schemes did not even know the personnel of extension agencies for their respective area. The rest 39 per cent of the sample farmers, although knew the personnel, were apparently not in receipt of any direct benefit from the extension service. Thus on the whole, the field survey shows the extension service under the schemes rather in poor light. Schemewise, the extension service appears to be somewhat better in Duliabam and Chenga whereas it is poor in schemes Sessa and Kaldiya.

Table 5.17 shows that compared to the farmers under government irrigation schemes, the farmers under STWs have better contact with the extension agencies. About 80 per cent of the sample farmers under STWs had good or very good contact with the extension agencies and were also benefited from the service. All the sample farmers under STWs know the personnel of extension agencies for their respective areas. About 19 per cent of the sample farmers,

Table 5.17 : Distribution of Sample Farmers under Different Private Irrigation Schemes according to the Level of Contact with Extension Agencies

Level of Contact \ Locations	Dihing Thekerani	Panigaon Kalakhowa	Katimari Grant	Gotonga	Keotkuchi	Domoni	Total
(1)	(2)	(3)	(4)	(5)	(6)	(7)	(8)
Very good	0	0	6	6	1	2	15 (22.39)
Good	10	7	6	6	5	5	39 (58.21)
Moderate	1	4	0	0	5	3	13 (19.41)
Poor	0	0	0	0	0	0	0 (0.00)
Total	11	11	12	12	11	10	67 (100.00)

Note : Figures in parentheses represent percentages of total sample.

although knew the personnel, were apparently not in receipt of any direct benefit from the extension service. Thus on the whole, the sample survey shows the extension service under the schemes in a very good shape. Districtwise, the extension service appears to be very good in Nagaon which is followed by Barpeta and Dibrugarh districts. The better contact of the government extension agencies with the farmers under STWs may be because of operation of these schemes by Agriculture Department. Private shallow tube wells in the state are being provided by the Department of Agriculture under the scheme of *'Samriddha Krishak Yojana'* whereas government sector major, medium and minor schemes are being installed by Irrigation Department. Extension Agencies and Agriculture Department are very closely associated whereas Irrigation Department and Extension Agencies are not. Therefore, there seems to be better contact of the farmers under private irrigation with extension agencies compared to the government schemes.

5.11 Principal Findings of the Chapter

1. Utilisation rate under privately owned shallow tube wells is found to be higher than that under government irrigation. There is, however, variation in this rate across locations. Utilisation rate in privately owned schemes seems to be constrained somewhat by fragmentation and small size of holdings.
2. There is marked variation in the availability of irrigation water in the field depending on the type of irrigation schemes under which the farm operates. On the whole, 61 per cent of the sample farmers under government schemes received water as per requirement, whereas 82 per cent of the farmers operating under private schemes received the same. Clearly, the performance of the privately owned shallow tube well schemes has been superior to that of government owned schemes as far as catering water according to the requirements of the farmers. Even within government sector, under the major and medium schemes sharp variations in water availability in different reaches of the command area were observed. In case of government minor schemes such variations were not pronounced.
3. The factors responsible for non-availability of water at proper times and consequent underutilisation of irrigation potential created under government owned schemes have been found to be largely supply side related. The problems faced are mainly the problem of irregular supply of electricity and mechanical defect in the motors, especially in the case of lift irrigation schemes, poor canal system, broken canal structure leading to waterlogging in the low-lying areas, non-availability of fund for maintenance etc.

Lack of coordination among different departments involved in providing irrigation water to the field is another problem particularly for the lift irrigation schemes.

4. The privately owned shallow tube well schemes are generally free from such supply side factors afflicting the government schemes which explains the better utilisation rates of private schemes. In other words, the better performance of private minor schemes in supplying irrigation water to fields as per requirement can be attributed mainly to a better maintenance and management of these schemes.
5. The efficiency of the government schemes can also be enhanced a lot if the water using farmers can be involved in the maintenance and management of the schemes. It was observed that Mandia minor scheme under Barpeta district could provide irrigation water to about 91.67 per cent of the sample farmers as per their requirements. Interestingly day-to-day maintenance and operation of this scheme are taken care of by the *Pathar Parichalana Samiti* (Field Management Committee) of the area. Thus involvement of the farmers in management of the schemes may be one important factor in better utilisation of irrigation water.
6. The average cropping intensity was 159 per cent in case of farms under government irrigation schemes while for privately owned shallow tube wells it was 197 per cent. Thus it is obvious that private irrigation schemes have performed better than government schemes in practicing multiple cropping.
7. The use of HYVs is almost universal in the sense that more than 90 per cent of the sample farmers are found to be using them. However, the proportion of HYV area in the total rice acreage still remains limited to

only 58.24 per cent in case of government schemes and 51.02 per cent for private shallow tube wells.

8. The average rate of fertilizer consumption estimated for the sample area was found to be much higher than the figure reported for the state in 1999-2000. Higher fertilizer consumption in the sample area is to be expected as the sample includes only irrigated farms. But the important thing to note is that with availability of irrigation farmers in Assam also use fertilizers at rates comparable to agriculturally advanced regions of India. On the average, farmers under private irrigation applied fertilizer at a higher dose than farmers under government irrigation. There are, however, instances of using overdoses of fertilizer in the sample farms.
9. The yield of rice at 25.73 quintal per hectare for government schemes and 26.37 quintal per hectare for private schemes are found to be much higher than the average yield of rice for the state as a whole. This figure can compare favourably with the average yield of rice in states like Haryana, Andhra Pradesh, Karnataka, etc.
10. Better utilisation of irrigation water under privately owned shallow tube wells has a direct relation with extension network. The field survey shows that extension service in case of privately owned shallow tube wells is far better compared to the government irrigation schemes. While 35 per cent of the farmers under government sector are directly benefited by the extension service, the proportion of farmers getting direct benefit from extension service is more than double at about 80 per cent. The difference may be due to the fact that the private STW schemes are installed with active facilitation by the State Agriculture Department which also provides the extension service.

5.12 Conclusion

The above discussion shows that utilisation rate in case of privately owned schemes is much better than the government owned and operated schemes. The effectiveness in using productivity raising practices, namely, multiple cropping, crop diversification, use of soil nutrients, etc. is also found to be better for farmers under private irrigation. The factors behind underutilisation of irrigation potential under different irrigation forms have also been broadly identified. However, to be able to ascertain the causes of underutilisation of irrigation potential under different conditions, further and more in-depth analysis is required. Accordingly, a detailed case study of selected irrigation schemes representing different conditions has been carried out. The findings of the exercise are presented and discussed in the next chapter.

REFERENCE

CMIE (2001), *Basic Statistics Relating to Indian Economy : Agriculture*, Centre for Monitoring Indian Economy, Mumbai, November.

APPENDIX 5.A

The Method of Processing Farmers' Responses Towards Extension Services

The following questions were asked to know the extent of farmers' direct contact with the government agencies :

(a) Do you know the VLEW of your village?
Yes (1)/ No (0)
(If the answer is No proceed to e)

(b) Have you consulted him on farming problems recently?
Yes (1)/ No (0)

(c) How many times during the last season?

(d) Have you followed his advice?
(i) Did not follow (0).
(ii) Followed but found useless (1).
(iii) Followed and found useful (2).

(e) Do you know the AEO of your area?
Yes (1)/ No (0)

(f) Did he visit your village during the last three months?
Yes (1)/ No (0)

Figures in the parentheses represent respective code. On the basis of score, four classes were categorised as follows :

(1) Very good – score 6
(2) Good – score 3 to 5
(3) Moderate – score 1 and 2
(No help received but knew VLEW/AEO)
(4) Poor – score 0
(Did not know VLEW/AEO)

6

Factors Behind Low Utilisation of Irrigation Potential

In the previous chapter the difference in efficiency of utilisaiton and effectiveness in use of better farming practices across farms operating under different types of irrigation have been presented. The analysis in the chapter has indicated the factors lying behind the differences in the efficiency and effectiveness of different types of irrigation schemes. In this chapter, a closer examination of conditions under different irrigation forms is taken up with the objective of ascertaining the factors responsible for low utilisation of irrigation potential. The methodology adopted for the purpose is the case study method. For the case study, a sub-sample of projects representing different size, techno-physical types and ownership has been selected. For each of these schemes, the utilisation rate and the specific conditions accounting for the observed utilisation rate have been sorted out. The factors responsible for unsatisfactory utilisation of created irrigation potential in the state have then been inferred by generalising from the commonalities and the contrasts observed in the specific conditions of different irrigation schemes.

6.1 Major and Medium Schemes

Out of a total of 19 existing major and medium irrigation

schemes in the state the two taken for the purpose of field investigation are Jamuna from Nagaon District and Kaldiya from Barpeta District. Jamuna is one of the two completed major schemes in the state whereas Kaldiya is a medium scheme. In the following sections, an attempt has been made to identify the factors responsible for the observed utilisation rates in these two schemes.

6.1.1 Jamuna Irrigation Project

It may be recalled that Jamuna Irrigation Project is the largest irrigation scheme in the state completed so far. It has an estimated irrigation potential of 30,996 hectares. Jamuna is the first medium flow irrigation venture in Assam, located primarily in the southern part of Nagaon District. It is a run of the river diversion system commissioned in 1969 with a culturable command area of 27705.66 hectares. It is designed to tap the water resources of Jamuna river near Bakuliaghat by construction of Main Weir, Head Regulator, and Guide Bunds, which facilitated the diversion of the river flow to the canal system. The project has a canal network of 264.63 km with 3 (three) major distributaries and a number of minors, sub-minors and water courses.

The project report was initially prepared by Central Water and Power Commission (CWPC) in 1959-60 after carrying out survey in the region where the project is implemented. Besides the CWPC, The Geological Survey of India carried out geological study and the Directorate of River Research Station, State PWD (Flood Control and Irrigation Department) carried out soil exploration of the headworks site. The model study of the headworks was designed by the Central Water and Power Research Station, Poona in 1964. The final survey of the canal system and design of the canal system was carried out by the State Engineers of the PWD (Flood Control & Irrigation Department).

It may be noted that Jamuna Irrigation project is located

in the rain shadow area of Nagaon district and hence unlike in most other parts of the state, irrigation is required not only for the dry season *rabi* and pre-*kharif* crops, but also for the *kharif* crops.

For the purpose of conducting field study, three villages irrigated by D_3 distributary were selected, one each from the head, middle and tail reach. (The details of the villages selected are given in Table 4.1).

As mentioned above, the scheme has an estimated irrigation potential of 30,996 hectares. However, full utilisation of this estimated potential has not been possible. The utilisation of created irrigation potential in Jamuna Irrigation Scheme for the year 2000-01 is shown in Table 6.1.

Table 6.1 : Utilisation of Irrigation Potential Created in Jamuna Irrigation Scheme

Estimated Potential (Area in Hectares)	*Potential Available for Utilisation (Area in Hectares)*	*Potential Utilised in 2000-01 (Area in Hectares)*	*Percentage of Utilisation*
30,996	30,996	20,744	66.92

Source : Statistical Cell, Irrigation Department, Government of Assam

Table 6.1 shows that the rate of utilisation of created irrigation potential in the scheme is quite good compared to the overall utilisation rate in the state. But there is still about thirty-three per cent of created irrigation potential which could not be utilised during the reference year. However, the underutilisation is due to supply side factors as farmers reported non-availability rather than non-necessity of irrigation as the factor for this.

The problem of non-availability of water is most marked in the tail reach of the project. Water is not available in adequate quantity in *rabi* and pre-*kharif* season and even in *kharif* season. Conveyance of water in the minors, sub-minors and water courses is not substantial. However, for middle and upper reach farmers availability of water during *kharif* season is not a problem. But for *rabi* and pre-*kharif* crops, supply of water in the middle reach is also not sufficient. Release of water for *rabi* and pre-*kharif* crops is late and so farmers raising *rabi* crops (particularly vegetables) have to supplement canal water by way of water from tube-wells. So far as the upper reaches are concerned, the north bank of the canal is getting water during both pre-*kharif* and *kharif* season. But the south bank of the canal is high land and is not getting water. Farmers in the middle and tail reaches complain of the resistance of farmers in upper reach people in releasing water. However, this problem is not unique to Jamuna Project alone. Similar type of incident has been reported by Mitra (1984) while carrying out a study in Mula Irrigation Project in Maharashtra.

To verify the complaints of the farmers regarding variation of water availability in different reaches of the project, an attempt was made to compute the total irrigated area of the sample farms and also area irrigated per hectare of operational holding at different reaches of the project. The results are presented in Table 6.2.

Table 6.2 : Area Irrigated per Hectare of Operational Holding at Different Reaches of Jamuna Irrigation Scheme

Sl. No.	*Reach*	*Area Irrigated per Hectare of Operational Holding*
(1)	*(2)*	*(3)*
1	Head	1.41
2	Middle	1.62
3	Tail	0.48
4	overall	1.11

Table 6.2 shows that there is considerable variation at different reaches of the scheme so far as irrigated area per hectare of operational holding is concerned. While the

farmers at head and middle reaches had more than 1.40 hectares of irrigated area per hectare of operational holding, the farmers at tail reaches had only 0.48 hectares of irrigated area per hectare of operational holding. This is far below the average irrigated area per hectare of operational holding at 1.10. Irrigated area per hectare of operational holding is the highest in the middle reach of the project at 1.62. This is followed by farmers in the head reach where irrigated area as proportion to operational holding is 1.41. Thus, the performance of the scheme can be considered the best at the middle reach of the project. The scheme performs very badly towards the tail reach of the command area.

The factors responsible for the project authority not being able to provide irrigation have been identified as the following. The identification is based on inputs provided by sample farmers and the officials administering the project. The responses from both the sides are used for cross-checking their mutual responses and drawing the scholar's own inferences in this regard.

(i) Lack of Proper Maintenance of the Distributary Network

Due to lack of maintenance, many of the branch canals, minors, sub-minors and water courses used to carry water to field are damaged resulting in non-availability of water in the field at the time of requirement. Even a small repairing work could not be undertaken by the Department due to paucity of fund. As a result, some areas are experiencing waterlogging while some other areas are not getting water in sufficient quantity. Thirty per cent of the sample farmers in tail reach of the scheme reported this to be one of the reasons for underutilisation of capacity created.

(ii) Faulty Design of the Canals

Twenty-one per cent of the farmers in the tail reach of the

project reported that due to faulty alignment and defective construction some water courses were never able to provide irrigation water. It is also observed that the canal system in the canal area is mostly unlined field canals. This results in conveyance loss of water.

(iii) Encroachment of the Command Area

In many parts of the command area in the tail reach, inhabitation of people has taken place affecting the minors, sub-minors and water courses in the area. Ultimately, this has resulted in non-availability of water by farmers in the command area. This problem has been reported by about 30 per cent of the sample farmers in the tail reach of the project.

(iv) Problem of Floods

Some of the areas in the lower reach of the project are regularly flooded by the Dimoru river in the *kharif* season. This has resulted damage not only to crops but also to the canal system in the area. This particular problem has been referred to by about 20 per cent of the farmers in the tail reach of the command area as one of the factors for underutilisation of potential of the project.

Although these factors are contributing immensely towards underutilisation of potential of the project, there are some good aspects of the scheme as well. It is worth mentioning that the problem of underutilisation is most marked in the lower reach of the scheme only. In the upper and middle reach of the project, the problem is not so acute. In fact, availability of water in these two reaches, in general, is fairly satisfactory. The relatively better performance of the scheme, can be attributed to — (a) active association of the Field Management Committees (FMC) in water distribution matters, and (b) closer coordination between the farmers and the irrigation departmental officials.

The experience from Jamuna Project thus points towards a conclusion that failure in utilisation of irrigation potential arises mainly from lack of maintenance which is accentuated by dearth of fund. Faulty design of the canals is also partly responsible for failure to utilise full irrigation potential. However, involvement of farmers' associations in the management of water distribution contributes towards better utilisation.

6.1.2 Kaldiya Irrigation Project

Kaldiya Irrigation Project is a medium irrigation scheme located in the district of Barpeta. The headwork of the scheme is at a place called Rehabari on river Kaldiya. The scheme was started in the year 1975-76 at an estimated cost of Rs. 8.11 crore and at present about ninety-nine per cent work of the project is completed. Apart from a main canal, there are 8-branch canals for providing irrigation water to the field. However, there are some problems with branch canal no. 7 and these are yet to be solved. The estimated potential of the scheme is 16,500 hectares of which 9,716 hectares are for *kharif* crops and the rest 6,784 hectares for *rabi* and pre-*kharif* crops. However, potential available for utilisation is much lower than the estimated potential. The yearwise potential available for irrigation and utilisation thereof for the three years starting from 1999-2000 is given in Table 6.3.

Table 6.3 : Irrigation Potential Available and Utilised in Kaldiya Irrigation Project

Year	*Estimated Potential (Area in hectares)*	*Potential Available for Irrigation (Area in hectares)*	*Potential Utilised (Area in hectares)*	*Percentage of Utilisation*
(1)	*(2)*	*(3)*	*(4)*	*(5)*
1999-2000	16,500	15,250	2,242	14.70
2000-2001	16,500	15,250	3,165	20.75
2001-2002	16,500	12,470	2,391	19.17

Source: Office of the Executive Engineer, Irrigation Department, Pathsala Division.

Table 6.3 shows that rate of utilisation under the scheme is very low. More than 80 per cent of the amount available for utilisation has remained unutilised for almost all these three years.

As in the case of Jamuna, lack of utilisation is due to supply side factors as it was found that enough water was not available to meet the farmers' requirements of irrigation water. Although the scheme is designed to cater to the needs of the farmers both in *kharif* and *rabi* season, water can be made available to the field only in the *kharif* season. Availability of water in the river during *rabi* season is very less and as such sufficient water to the field cannot be supplied for the purpose of irrigation. Again, water is available only in the main canal. The branch canals do not get sufficient water and as a result the farmers in the command area nearer to the branch canals do not get sufficient water for irrigation. The following factors are identified as contributing to the underutilisation of irrigation potential of the scheme.

(i) Lack of Maintenance of Canals

About 47 per cent of the cultivators in the command area attribute underutilisation of created potential to lack of proper maintenance of the canal network. According to them, canals in the command area are either broken or damaged due to depreciation over the years. Seepage and leakage of irrigation water takes place through these broken parts of the canals. The gates in the canals controlling water were found to be either broken or reported to be stolen. As a result, while some of the cultivators are not getting sufficient water, some others are having their fields waterlogged. About 60 per cent of the sample farmers were found to be affected by this twin problem.

(ii) Absence of Land Levelling Works

In one of our field study sites, namely Tuplai-Panbari, it was found that one side of the command area was highland to which water cannot be flown. Obviously in such part of the command area water could not be supplied as land levelling work had not been carried out or completed.

Although the factors behind non-utilisation of irrigation potential in Kaldiya are similar to those in Jamuna, it is important to note that the problem is much more serious in Kaldiya. This can be attributed to the fact that the kind of positive coordination between the farming community and the irrigation department observed in Jamuna Project is virtually absent in Kaldiya. In the management of water distribution and maintenance the farming community is not involved and such work appears to be the sole responsibility of the government department which is perennially handicapped by lack of funds.

6.2 Government Minor Schemes

It may be recalled that a total of 1,568 minor irrigation schemes have been completed under government schemes in the state up to the end of 2000-01. Government minor irrigation schemes in the state are of different types including surface lift, ground water lift and surface flow. In case of surface lift irrigation schemes, water is lifted from surface water bodies like river, rivulet, *beel,* etc. with the help of electrical or diesel operated motors. Groundwater lift schemes in the state are of two types — deep tube-wells and shallow tube-wells. As the name suggests, while the deep tube-wells tap deep seated aquifers (more than 300 feet deep from the earth's surface), the shallow tube-wells tap shallow aquifers (less than 200 feet from the earth's surface). While the deep tube-wells are generally fitted with high power water lifting machines of more than 15 H.P. capacity, the shallow tube-wells are fitted with small power lifting machines of 3 to 5 H.P. capacity. The deep tube-wells, on an average, give a discharge of 1,35,000 litres per hour and have a command area of 80 to 100 hectares (Government of India, 1976).

Apart from heterogeneity in the nature of government irrigation schemes, the area irrigated by these schemes are also not uniform. The capacity of these schemes may vary from as low as 120 hectares to a maximum of 2000 hectares. However, the estimated potential of the government minor irrigation schemes are much more compared to the private minor schemes currently in operation in the state.

Five schemes from the currently operating government minor schemes in the districts of Dibrugarh and Barpeta were selected for our case study. These include four-surface lift irrigation schemes and one groundwater lift irrigation scheme. The schemes selected are Sessa LIS and Duliabam LIS in Dibrugarh District and Chenga DTW, Mandia LIS and Puthimari LIS in Barpeta District. In the following sections an attempt is made to identify the factors responsible for observed utilisation of created irrigation potential in each of these schemes.

6.2.1 Sessa LIS

Sessa is one of 27 completed minor irrigation schemes in Dibrugarh district. Located near Gamon bridge under Barbaruah Development Block the scheme is a surface lift irrigation scheme. Water is lifted from river Buridihing with the help of two barges. There are 7 electrical pumps of 40 H. P. each on full utilisation of which a total of 930 hectares of area can be brought under irrigation. This includes 600 hectares for *kharif* crops and 330 hectares for *rabi* crops. However, at present only 3 pumps are working and the rest four are out of order. The scheme was started in the year 1975-76 at an initial investment of Rs. 7.98 lakhs and was completed in 1984-85. Water is supplied to the field with the help of the main canal, 1 (one) branch canal and minors. The total length of the canal is 8.5 km. out of which 3910 metres have the provision of lining. The length of the main, branch canal and the minor are 4 km., 2.5 km. and 2 km. respectively. The villages included under the command area of the scheme are Kotoha, Kotoha Borbil, Kotoha Nagaon, Mazgaon, Kotoha Bengali Gaon, etc. Total number of beneficiary households in 2000-01 was 128. Total potential created under the scheme up to the end of 2000-01 was 930 hectares. However utilisation of the said created potential was much less. Potential created and utilised under the scheme for last three years is given in Table 6.4.

Table 6.4 : Potential Created and Utilised under Sessa LIS

Year	*Estimated Potential (Area in hectares)*	*Potential Created (Area in hectares)*	*Potential Utilised (Area in hectares)*	*Percentage of Utilisation*
(1)	*(2)*	*(3)*	*(4)*	*(5)*
1998-1999	930	930	180	19.36
1999-2000	930	930	104	11.18
2000-2001	930	930	170	18.28

Source : Office of the Executive Engineer, Irrigation, Dibrugarh.

It is clear from Table 4.6 that the rate of utilisation for the scheme is very dismal. More than 81 per cent of the potential created remained unutilised in 2000-01. As in both the major and medium cases discussed above, the low utilisation of irrigation potential in the scheme is clearly due to supply side failure as more than half of the pumping capacity is out of operation due to mechanical failure. The factors for poor utilisation of irrigation capacity have been identified as the following :

(i) Absence of Mechanical Maintenance

As reported above, more than half of the capacity was not available for utilisation in the reference year due to mechanical breakdown of four out of seven pumps of the whole irrigation system. The pumps reportedly remained unrepaired as government could not make the necessary fund available for repairing.

(ii) Erratic Supply of Electricity

Sessa is a lift irrigation scheme where water is lifted from river Buridihing with the help of electrically operated motors. So, the role of electricity in full utilisation of irrigation potential of the scheme is very crucial. However, erratic power supply has been found to be a factor responsible for non-availability of water in time. Twenty per cent of sample farmers have reported that supply of irrigation water to their fields was adversely affected due to irregularity of electricity supply.

(iii) Lack of Maintenance of Canal Network

As in the case of major and medium schemes, lack of maintenance of canal network has been found to be a factor for non-utilisation of available irrigation water in the scheme. Sixty per cent of sample farmers have been found to report that availability of water to their fields has been affected due to lack of proper maintenance of the canals. Lack of maintenance for years together has resulted in damaged and broken canals leading to leakage of water. Thus, some of the areas in the command area do not get water in right time and in adequate quantity whereas some other get excess water leading to waterlogging and damage to crops.

(iv) Conveyance Loss

About forty per cent of the cultivators opined that the farmers in the tail reach do not get sufficient water for irrigation because of conveyance loss. Some portions of the branch canal (after 1210 metres) are earthen where seepage of water takes place leading to non-availability of water by farmers in the tail reach.

(v) Lack of Coordination among Various Departments

About ten per cent of the sample farmers in the command area of the scheme also reported about the lack of coordination between Irrigation Department and the Assam State Electricity Board (ASEB) for underutilisation of irrigation potential in the scheme. This problem, however, is not unique to Sessa LIS only. Gogoi (1989) found this to be a major problem in full utilisation of irrigation potential in Jorhat district of Assam. Programme Evaluation Organisation of the Planning Commission (1966) has also observed this to be a major factor contributing to underutilisation of irrigation potential in some of the major irrigation projects in the country.

(vi) Lack of Involvement of the Farming Community in Management

The scheme has been found to be fully owned and operated by the government only. In no work of the scheme the farmers were found to be involved. As such coordination between the farmers and the government is also found to be absent.

There is also no provision of collecting water charge from the beneficiary farmers.

6.2.2 Duliabam LIS

This is a river lift irrigation scheme located under Khowang Development Block in Dibrugarh district. Originally started as a point of Khowang LIS by the Department of Agriculture, the scheme was later handed over to Irrigation Department. The scheme was remodelled in the year 1999-2000 by the Department and now it is an independent scheme. Started in 1971-72 at an initial investment of Rs. 22.20 lakh, it was completed in the year 1973-74. Water is lifted from river Dimow with the help of three electric motors of 20 H.P. each although the original provision was to install 5 pumps of 20 H.P. each. The command area of the scheme consists of three villages, namely Duliabam, Dulia Lahowal and 11/164 ORR Grant and beneficiaries belong to Ahom and Chutia community. There is one main canal and a branch canal carrying water to the field. The estimated length of the main and branch canal are 2700 metres and 1320 metres respectively out of which 1500 metres of the main and 1000 metres of the branch canal have the lining provision. The estimated potential of the scheme is 140 hectares of which 105 hectares are for *kharif* and 35 hectares for *rabi* and pre-*kharif* crops. However, utilisation of created potential in the scheme is much lower. Utilisation of potential created in the scheme with effect from 1998-99 is shown in Table 6.5.

Table 6.5 : Utilisation of Irrigation Potential Created in Duliabam LIS

Year	*Estimated Potential (Area in hectares)*	*Potential Created up to the Year (Area in hectares)*	*Potential Utilised During the Year (Area in hectares)*	*Percentage of Utilisation*
(1)	*(2)*	*(3)*	*(4)*	*(5)*
1998-1999	140	140	24	17.15
1999-2000	140	140	50	35.71
2000-2001	140	140	55	39.29

Source : Office of the Executive Engineer, Irrigation, Dibrugarh Division.

Thus, it is evident from Table 6.5 that as in the case of other irrigation schemes under investigation, in Duliabam also potential created could not be fully utilised. In fact, the rate of utilisation in the scheme is relatively low. However, the rate has significantly improved since 1999-2000, the year in which remodelling of the scheme was done. While the utilisation rate of the scheme more than doubled in the year 1999-2000 over the previous year, the rate improved further to 39.29 per cent in 2000-01, the latest year for which utilisation statistics is available. The factors hindering the utilisation of the scheme in the field level are given below. These could be identified while interviewing the farmers in the command area of the scheme.

(i) Absence of Mechanical Maintenance

The scheme has a provision of 5 (five) electrical pumps on full functioning of which a potential of 140 hectares could be made available for utilisation. However, only three pumps are functioning at present and the rest two cannot be operated due to some mechanical defect. Thus the potential available for utilisation is also reduced considerably.

(ii) Irregular Supply of Electricity

For providing irrigation water to the field, regular supply of electricity is most important. But 30 per cent of the sample farmers in the command area reported that supply of electricity in the scheme was the most irregular. Sometimes, the voltage was also not sufficient for continuous lifting of water. Thus the farmers cannot always expect irrigation water at the time of their requirement because of erratic supply of electricity.

(iii) Conveyance Loss

The scheme has a provision of one main canal and a branch canal for distribution of irrigation water. However, the entire length of the canals do not have the lining provision. The earthen portion of the canals experience lots of seepage and substantial conveyance loss leading to underutilisation of created irrigation potential. About 50 per cent of the farmers interviewed in the command area of the scheme reported this problem and the officials in-charge of the scheme also agreed to this.

As in the case of Sessa, farmers' participation in the operation and maintenance of the scheme was not observed in this scheme. The farmers' associations like the Field Management Committee (FMC) were not found to be active in the command area of the scheme. As in most of the government owned schemes, the maintenance and operation of this scheme also is fully contributed by the State Irrigation Department.

In spite of these similarities, comparatively better utilisation in this scheme than in Sessa appears to be due to the fact that the canals are in much better condition in this case. The canal network in this scheme was newly laid when the scheme was remodelled in 1999-2000. Thus the problem of maintenance of the canals has not yet surfaced.

6.2.3 Mandia LIS

Out of total 11 completed minor irrigation schemes in Barpeta subdivision of the district, Mandia LIS is a functioning scheme. The scheme has two extensions—extension old and extension new. Extension old has two points at Bhatkuchi while extension new has one point at Kopoha. Kopoha point of Mandia LIS was taken for field study. The scheme was started in the financial year 1981-82. Water is lifted from the river Bhelengi (also known as Pahumara) with the help of two electric motors from a barge in the river. The river is a perennial one, and so there is no difficulty in lifting water during winter too. The scheme initially had three motors on running of which total potential created amounted to around

200 hectares. The day to day maintenance of the scheme has now been left to the Field Management Committee (FMC) of the village which was formed in the year 1987-88. The command area of the scheme is a low-lying one which is flooded by the water of river Pahumara during summer. The farmers, therefore, cannot raise more than one crop. Summer paddy is the main crop practised in the command area. HYV seeds are used by the farmers. Popular varieties used include TTB, Pusa, Mahnsuri, etc. The yield of rice in the area is very good. It ranges between 40 to 45 quintal per hectare. Use of chemical fertilizer and other inputs of new technology are most common in the area. Soil lining, use of pesticides are also done by the farmers. All the benefited farmers under the command area are of immigrant origin including both Hindus and Muslims.

The estimated potential of the scheme is 200 hectares which, however, cannot be achieved due to a number of factors. Potential created and its utilisation for the scheme for last three years is given in Table 6.6.

Table 6.6 : Potential created and Utilised in Mandia Irrigation Scheme

Year	*Estimated Potential (Area in hectares)*	*Potential Created (Area in hectares)*	*Potential Utilised (Area in hectares)*	*Percentage of Utilisation*
(1)	*(2)*	*(3)*	*(4)*	*(5)*
1998-1999	200	200	50	25
1999-2000	200	200	50	25
2000-2001	200	200	61	30.5

Source : Office of the Executive Engineer (Irrigation), Barpeta Division, Sorbhog.

Table 6.6 shows that the rate of utilisation under the scheme is apparently low. However, in this case, it is to be noted that the demand for irrigation exists only in one season because the command area of the scheme is chronically flood prone in *kharif* season. Irrigation is required and utilised only in the flood-free season, but the irrigation available for *kharif* season cannot be utilised. If one discounts for this extreme seasonality of irrigation demand, the utilisation rate appears to be much better.

After interaction with the farmers in the command area of the scheme, following factors were found to be contributing to the underutilisation of the irrigation potential of the scheme :

(i) Absence of Mechanical Maintenance

Initially, there was a provision for three motors of 20 H.P. capacity each to lift water from the river. But at the time of field visit only two motors were found in operational stage. Similarly, the pipes in the barge were found broken which led to leakage of water. Thus, the full potential created were not available for utilisation.

(ii) Irregular Supply of Electricity

Water from river Pahumara is lifted with the help of two electrically operated motors of 20 H.P. capacity each. However, the supply of electricity in the scheme is not uninterrupted and the voltage is also not good. About 20 per cent of the beneficiary farmers in the command area of the scheme had reported this to be one of the major factors for under- utilisation of the created capacity.

(iii) Lack of Maintenance in the Distributary Network

As in the case of most of the other irrigation schemes in the state, Mandia scheme has also problems in the distributary network of the scheme. About 20 per cent of the beneficiary farmers reported that canals towards the end of the command area were broken due to which leakage of water took place depriving farmers in those areas from sufficient water for irrigation. This is mainly because of lack of maintenance of the scheme by the government. Although the FMC in the area is actively involved in maintenance and management of the scheme, due to paucity of funds, it has also failed to undertake major repairing work of the distributary network. As a result underutilisation of created potential has taken place.

However, there are certain positive aspects of the scheme because of which it has been performing relatively well in spite of its limitations.

The farmers' organisation in the form of Field Management Committee (FMC) was formed way back in 1987-88 and is fairly strong and firmly rooted now. The Committee is actively involved in management of distribution of water to the field. The Committee also sees that water supply is not affected due to non-attendance to minor maintenance jobs. It carries out such maintenance activities and funds the same by raising the necessary amount from its members. Carrying out such activity by the Committee has been possible because of good coordination between the farmers' associations and the government departments. Since farmers here can raise only one major crop, that too in the dry season, their stakes are high in keeping the irrigation system functioning. The Field Management Committee has been successful in channelising farmers' eagerness positively and productively.

However, the Committees are not equipped to handle major maintenance work. Hence, as in other government schemes, the major maintenance works remain unattended due to lack of fund with the Government Irrigation Department.

6.2.4 Chenga DTW

This DTW scheme is located under Chenga Development Block in Barpeta district. Two points of the scheme are presently working, one at Khongra and the other at Musalmanpara. Out of these two, the point at Musalmanpara was taken up for fieldwork. Water is carried to the field with the help of a main canal and a branch canal. However, the main canal is at present out of order and water is supplied only with the help of the branch canal. The point under study has been functioning well only since 1994-95. The Field Management Committee (FMC) in the village was constituted in the year 1996-97 and at present the FMC has been looking after the operation of the scheme. The estimated potential of the scheme is 60 hectares. Utilisation of potential created under the scheme for last three years is given in Table 6.7.

Table 6.7 : Potential Created and utilised Under Chenga DTW Scheme

Year	*Estimated Potential (Area in hectares)*	*Potential Created (Area in hectares)*	*Potential Utilised (Area in hectares)*	*Percentage of Utilisation*
(1)	(2)	(3)	(4)	(5)
1998-1999	60	60	5.00	8.33
1999-2000	60	60	22.50	37.50
2000-2001	60	60	25.50	42.50

Source: Office of the Executive Engineer (Irrigation), Barpeta Division, Sorbhog

It is clear from Table 6.7 that the rate of utilisation of the scheme as percentage of potential created is reasonably good. However, there is enough scope for improving this rate of utilisation. An attempt was made to find out the factors affecting utilisation of created potential in the scheme on the basis of information gathered from the sample farmers during field visit. The responses of the farmers can be described as given below :

(i) Absence of Mechanical Maintenance

Though not like lift irrigation schemes, Chenga DTW is also

affected by mechanical problems. The main switch of the pump set with the help of which water is extracted, itself has got some problems. It has resulted in difficulties in lifting water.

(ii) Irregular Supply of Electricity

As is mentioned earlier, supply of electricity is one crucial factor in full utilisation of potential created not only in surface lift irrigation schemes, but also in groundwater lift schemes. But supply of electricity in the scheme is found to be very irregular. About 40 per cent of the sample farmers reported that underutilisation in the scheme is taking place because of this factor also.

(iii) Lack of Maintenance of Canal Network

Although there is a provision of one main canal and a branch canal for the scheme, only the branch canal is at present working. The major portion of the main canal is virtually out of order. It has lots of holes resulting in leakage of water. As such the main canal cannot be used for carrying water to the field. Again, due to lack of maintenance on the part of the government, the distributary network of the scheme is getting worsened day by day.

However, as in the case of Mandia LIS, the Field Management Committee (FMC) in the area has been undertaking minor maintenance works which explains a better utilisation rate in the scheme compared to many others.

6.2.5 Puthimari LIS

This is a surface lift irrigation scheme under Gobardhana Development Block in Barpeta district. It is situated in a village called Puthimari about 4 km. towards east of Sorbhog town. The scheme was started in the year 1987 at an estimated cost of Rs. 7,85,000 and was completed in the year 1989. Water is lifted from a *beel* called Sorbhog *beel* with the help of 2 (two) electrically operated pumps of 20 H.P. capacity each. However, at present only one of the two pumps is functioning. Water is carried to the field with the help of a main canal. There is no provision of branch canal in the scheme. The potential of the scheme was estimated at 40 hectares of gross cropped area (GCA).

Winter paddy is the principal crop raised in the area. However, with the availability of irrigation water other crops like vegetables, wheat, pulses, oilseeds and autumn paddy are also raised in substantial quantities.

According to the farmers in the command area, the scheme is a good one but its performance can be made better by taking suitable measures. The potential created in the scheme and utilisation thereof with effect from 1998-99 are given in Table 6.8.

Table 6.8 : Potential Created and Utilised under Puthimari Irrigation Scheme in Different Years

Year	*Estimated Potential (Area in hectares)*	*Potential Created (Area in hectares)*	*Potential Utilised (Area in hectares)*	*Percentaget of Utilisation*
(1)	*(2)*	*(3)*	*(4)*	*(5)*
1998-1999	40	40	13	32.50
1999-2000	40	40	18	45.00
2000-2001	40	40	16.5	41.25

Source : Office of the Executive Engineer, Barpeta Division, Sorbhog.

The observed rate of utilisation of the irrigation potential created calls for identifying the factors behind it. Accordingly by interviewing the farmers in the command area, an attempt was made to identify the factors responsible for low utilisation of irrigation potential created.

(i) Mechanical Defect

The initial provision for lifting water in the scheme was of two electrical pumps of 20 H.P. each. However, due to some mechanical problems in one of them, only one pump is operating at present. Accordingly, availability of water in the field is also reduced.

(ii) Absence of Sub-canal

The entire command area of the scheme is yet to be irrigated because of absence of a sub-canal. There is only the main canal supplying water to the field which is not sufficient for the entire command area. About 80 per cent of the sample farmers interviewed cited this to be a cause for underutilisation of irrigation potential in the scheme.

(iii) Lack of Proper Maintenance of the Distributary Network

All the farmers interviewed in the command area of the scheme are of the view that lack of proper maintenance of the distributary network has contributed to the problem of underutilisation of irrigation potential. Due to non-repairing of the distributary canals, leakage of water has taken place leading to non-availability of sufficient water in the tail reach of the command area.

(iv) Faulty Design

A portion of the command area was found to be highland. In the absence of proper land levelling and other related works, this portion of the command area does not get sufficient water for irrigation. About 20 per cent of the farmers interviewed in the command area of the scheme referred to this as a factor for low utilisation of irrigation water in the scheme.

Thus the factors cited for underutilisation of potential created in the scheme are found to be design related, management and maintenance related and also related with absence of preparatory works. However, the scholar's observation is that some of these problems could have been solved with a better relationship between the government and the farming community. The kind of involvement of the farmers in the management and maintenance of the scheme seen in Mandia and Chenga was not observed in this location.

In spite of the usual problems and absence of involvement of the farming community in management, the utilisation rate is not among the worst. What seems to have helped in achieving the observed level of utilisation is the small scale nature of this scheme. Because of the small size, it could be managed more effectively by the departmental agency even without significant involvement of the farming community.

There is no provision of collecting water charge. The mood of the farmers regarding payment of levy is positive but they want the supply of water to be regular.

6.3 Constraints on Fuller Utilisation of Irrigation Potential in Private Minor Schemes

As shown in Table 5.1 in the previous chapter, the utilisation rate of privately owned shallow tube-wells is much better than that of the government owned and operated schemes. These schemes are generally free from factors such as lack of maintenance, faulty design, erratic supply of electricity afflicting the utilisation rates in government owned schemes. Yet the overall rate of utilisation of 51.92 per cent of these schemes, need to be bettered for improving the returns on investment on irrigation. The utilisation of irrigation potential created under these STWs is restrained mainly by the fragmented and small size of holdings.

Most of the farmers possessing STWs do not have the compact minimum area of land required for maximum utilisation of the potential created. As such, fullest utilisation of the created potential of STWs has not been possible. For example, in Katimari Grant in Nagaon District, none of the farmers possessing STWs has compact area of land as large as 2 hectares. In fact, about seventy-one per cent of the farmers possessing STWs and surveyed in the village have operational holdings less than the full capacity of the pump sets. This is not peculiar only for farmers in Katimari Grant but also has been equally observed for farmers in the other villages of the three districts taken for fieldwork. In such fragmented holdings, utilisation of maximum capacity of shallow tube-wells is not possible.

However, one positive development in this context is the emergence of the water market in a few locations in Dibrugarh and Nagaon districts of the field study. This phenomenon seems to have facilitated fuller utilisation of irrigation potential created.[1] In such areas farmers owning pumpset and having excess capacity due to small size of their holdings have been found to supply irrigation water to neighbouring farmers who on their own do not have the infrastructure for the purpose. Once such markets take root, farmers with excess irrigation capacity will be able to utilise it and farmers for whom setting up of pumpsets is not viable, can procure the necessary irrigation facility from the market. Development of water market, thus, can on one hand contribute towards better utilisation of installed irrigation capacity and on the other hand, can economise the total capital investment in private irrigation system.

As this market develops, certain regulations may become necessary to ensure that the market delivers the goods. Market facilitates optimum allocation of resources if it remains competitive. Thus steps will have to be taken to prevent the growth of monopolistic tendencies. Moreover, as of now, groundwater is an open access common property resource. Therefore, there is a danger of market-induced over-exploitation of this resource leading to the proverbial 'tragedy of commons' (Hardin, 1968). Groundwater based irrigation in such a situation may not be sustainable in the long run. Indeed in the context of a study in Bangladesh, Fujita and Hossain (1995) had also apprehended the possibility of over exploitation and depletion of the common property resource of groundwater because of growth of "private gains based market".

The regulations to avoid these problems may be in the form of specification of the size of the pump or in the number of pumps one can possess. (For example, one may not be allowed to install a very large capacity pump or a person already possessing a pump should not be allowed to have the second on subsidy).

6.4 Factors behind Low Utilisation of Irrigation Potential in the State

The discussion in the above sections leads to the following factors behind poor utilisation of irrigation projects in the state :

The main factor responsible for poor utilisation of government owned irrigation schemes is lack of maintenance. Maintenance works apparently suffer because government agencies generally lack the funds for carrying out such works.

Another problem contributing to low utilisation of irrigation potential in the government sector is lack of co-ordination between various agencies, such as different wings of the State Irrigation Department, the State Electricity Board etc. involved in delivering irrigation water to the field. This problem is endemic in all the lift irrigation schemes owned and operated by government agencies.

Faulty design of canals is also found to create problems in achieving fuller utilisation of irrigation potential in certain parts of command areas of a number of irrigation schemes in the government sector.

In certain parts of the command areas of some of the schemes, the necessary land levelling has not been carried out or completed. Consequently, these parts have not received irrigation water as projected in the initial project report.

Within the government owned schemes, utilisation rate is significantly higher in those schemes in which the co-ordination between the Irrigation Department and the farming community is better and farmers' associations like the Field Management Committees (FMCs) are involved in management of maintenance and distribution.

The privately owned shallow tube-wells are generally found to be free from the abovementioned factors afflicting government owned schemes which explains the better utilisation rate of private schemes.

For confirming the above observations extracted from the case studies, a regression analysis has also been carried out. Availability of water as per requirement to different clusters of sample farmers (as discussed in Chapter 5) is regressed to the extent of farmers' control in operation and management of the irrigation system. To distinguish between the three categories of (a) the least control of farmers in fully government owned and operated schemes, (b) moderate control of farmers in government owned schemes with farmers' participation in management and (c) fully controlled by farmers in private shallow tube-well schemes, two dummy variables have been used. These are—

D_1 = 1 if the cluster is from the command area of government irrigation schemes with participation of farmers in management, 0 otherwise.

D_2 = 1 if the cluster is irrigated by privately owned shallow tube-well systems, 0 otherwise.

The results of the regression analysis are presented in Table 6.9. Thus the constant term in the results of the analysis shown in Table 6.9, captures the mean availability in fully government owned operated sector; the coefficient of D_1 captures the difference in availability in government owned projects operated with farmers' participation in management over that in fully government owned operated sector; and the coefficient of D_2 captures the difference in availability in privately owned shallow tube-well sector over that in fully government owned operated sector.

Table 6.9 : Results of Regression Analysis of Availability of Water as per Requirement to Clusters of Sample Farmers

Variables	*Coefficients/ Values*	*Standard Error*
(1)	*(2)*	*(3)*
Constant	51.334***	4.921
D_1	29.501***	9.206
D_2	31.0666****	6.663
R^2	0.705	
F (n_1=2, n_2=10)	11.971***	

*** indicates significant at 0.01 level.

The regression gives a high R^2 value with highly significant F statistic for overall regression. The positive and highly significant coefficient of D_1 shows that efficiency in delivering water as per requirement is better under government owned schemes with farmers' participation in management than under totally government owned and controlled schemes. The larger and significant coefficient of D_2 shows that the efficiency is even better for privately owned and operated shallow tube-well schemes.

Though the observed rates of utilisation of the private shallow tube-wells are better, the rates are by no means nearly full. The fuller utilisation of irrigation potential created under these STWs has been found to be restrained mainly by the fragmented and small size of holdings. Most of the farmers possessing STWs do not have the compact minimum area of land required for maximum utilisation of the potential created. As a result, fullest utilisation of the created potential of STWs has not been possible.

To further ascertain this point, 'utilisation rate of privately owned shallow tube-well schemes' has been regressed to 'the largest compact plot in the operational holding of the farmer owning the system' (denoted in short as LCP). To control the influences of regional variation across the three districts from which the sample has been drawn, two dummy variables L_1 and L_2 have also been included as regressors. L_1 takes the value 1 for Nagaon and 0 for other two districts and L_2 takes the value 1 for Barpeta and 0 otherwise. Results are presented in Table 6.10.

Table 6.10 : Results of Regression Analysis of Utilisation Rates of Private Shallow Tube Well Schemes

Variables	*Coefficients/Values*	*Standard Error*
(1)	*(2)*	*(3)*
Constant	30.643***	8.110
LCP	9.947**	4.406
L_1	-3.861	8.645
L_2	17.071**	8.316
R^2	0.229	
F (n_1=3, n_2=56)	5.540***	

and * imply significance at 0.05 and 0.01 levels respectively .

Though the value of R^2 is not high, the F-statistic for overall regression and the coefficient of the variable the largest compact plot (LCP) are statistically significant. The positive sign of the coefficient of LCP means that bigger the largest compact plot of the owner farmer, better is the utilisation rate. In other words, small and fragmented holdings of owners hamper fuller utilisation of privately owned shallow tube-well schemes.

6.5. Conclusion

The foregoing analysis has confirmed that the poor utilisation rate of government owned irrigation schemes is predominantly a fall-out of inefficient management of projects manifested in absence of routine maintenance of machineries and distributary canals, failure in achieving coordination between various departments and branches involved in delivery of water, etc.

Collection of water levy is imperative for improving utilisation by carrying out the regular maintenance works. Since lack of fund allocation is the main factor hampering maintenance work, collection of water levy can generate the necessary fund for maintenance and operation. The farmers' responses in the field study showed that they were willing to pay the levy provided water is supplied to the field in time and in required quantity.

The privately owned shallow tube-wells are generally found to be free from such factors afflicting government schemes which explains the better utilisation rates observed in case of the former. The better performance of private minor schemes, thus, can be attributed mainly to better maintenance and management of these schemes.

However, there is scope to improve the rate of utilisation of private minor schemes as well. The main factor hindering full utilisation of irrigation capacity in case of these schemes is the non-availability of a minimum compact area for irrigation due to fragmentation of holdings. Hence, suitable land reform measures to consolidate the fragmented holdings can contribute to fuller utilisation of irrigation capacity of privately owned shallow tube-well schemes. However, emergence of groundwater market in certain areas has helped in better utilisation of irrigation potential in spite of predominance of small and fragmented holdings. Since such groundwater market can substitute not-too-easily implementable holding consolidation measures, development of such market should be facilitated. However, as the market is facilitated, there should also be adequate regulation and control to prevent the possible undesirable fall-out discussed above.

NOTE

1. In Katimari Grant of Nagaon district, water was found to be charged at the rate of 2 maunds (0.80 quintal) per bigha (0.13387 hectares) of land irrigated. In Dihing Thekerani in Dibrugarh district, there are instances of farmers with pumpsets providing irrigation water to other farmers in return of some benefit, though the concrete price formation as in Katimari Grant has not yet taken place.

REFERENCES

Fujita, K. and Hossain F. (1995), "Role of the Ground Water Market in Agricultural Development and Income Distribution : A Case Study in North West Bangladesh Village", *The Developing Economics*, XXXII-4.

Gogoi, K. (1989), "Irrigation in Assam" in P.C. Goswami (Ed.) (1989), *Agriculture in Assam*, Assam Institute of Development Studies, Guwahati.

Government of India (1966), *Evaluation of Major Irrigation Projects : Some Case Studies*, Programme Evaluation Organisation, Planning Commission.

Government of India (1976), *Report of the National Commission on Agriculture*, Part V, p. 20.

Hardin, Garrett (1968), "The Tragedy of Commons", *Science*, 162 [Reprinted in Sankar, U. (Ed.) *Environmental Economics* (2001), Oxford University Press].

Mitra, A. K. (1984), "Managing Irrigation System in Drought Prone Areas", *Indian Journal of Agricultural Economics*, Vol. 39, No. 3, July-September.

7

Irrigation Forms and Effectiveness in Use of Better Farming Practices

It may be recalled that some broad conclusions regarding effectiveness of different forms and types of irrigation schemes were drawn in chapter five as indicated by simple tools like ratios, averages, etc. But these conclusions based on ratios, averages, etc. may not be rigorous enough and may sometimes be misleading too. This is due to the fact that while comparing averages or ratios, other influencing factors are not necessarily kept constant or controlled. The apparent differences in averages or ratios, therefore, may be because of configuration of values of other factors. To be able to draw inferences in a more rigorous manner, multiple regression analyses have been carried out. The main purpose of such analysis was to see whether the use of productivity raising practices and inputs tend to differ significantly depending on the form of irrigation.

The summary findings reported in chapter five indicate that productivity raising farm practices tend to differ across farms according to whether it operates under government owned and managed irrigation system or privately owned systems. It was also observed that among farmers operating under government irrigation, there was clear difference to the extent of use of some of these practices depending on whether the farmers' associations were involved in the management of the schemes. Involvement of stake-holding farmers through farmers' associations in management give farmers better control on supply and timing of irrigation water enabling them for more extensive use of productivity raising farm practices. Accordingly, to accommodate these situations, irrigation projects were classified to distinguish between government irrigation schemes without involvement of farmers in management, government schemes with farmers' involvement in management and privately owned schemes.

Thus the projects included in the sample were classified into these three categories: (a) projects fully owned and managed by government agencies, (b) projects owned by government agencies whose management and operation are largely controlled by stake-holding farmers, and (c) owned and operated by the farmers. The projects in category (a) and (b) are relatively larger, each catering to a group of farmers. In case of category (b), the water using farmers are better organized through their Field Management Committees[1] (locally known as *Pathar Parichalana Samiti*) which provide a ready institution for controlling and managing water release and distribution. The category (c) projects are small, shallow tube-well (STW) based each capable of irrigating up to 2 hectares of land and usually owned and used individually by farmers. Of the total sample of 172 farmers, 62 get irrigation from category (a) projects, 43 from category (b) and 67 from category (c) projects.

7.1 Indicators of Effective Use of Irrigation

It is well-known that irrigation facilitates practice of multiple cropping, use of high yielding varieties (HYVs), application of fertilizers and achieving crop diversification. Hence, the extent of multiple cropping measured by cropping intensity

(CI), use of HYV seeds measured by proportion of HYV rice area in total rice acreage (HYV_R), fertilizer consumption in terms of kilograms of N+P+K per hectare of gross cropped area (FC) and crop diversification in two forms, namely (a) the proportion of area under non-rice crops in the GCA (CD_r) and (b) proportion of area under non-winter rice crops in gross cropped area (CD_w) have been taken as indicators of effective use of irrigation.

Keeping in view the locational contexts of the present study, yield of rice (Y_R), the principal crop of the area, has also been included as an additional indicator. Thus the indicators of effective use of irrigation are CI, HYV_R, FC, Y_R, CD_r and CD_w and they constitute endogenous variables for the econometric models.

7.2 Analysis of Multiple Cropping

The extent of multiple cropping is being measured by the cropping intensity, i.e. percentage of the gross cropped area of the farm to its net sown area and is denoted by the variable CI. The variation in cropping intensity across farms has been sought to be explained in terms of the following explanatory factors :

(a) Irrigation Form

The summary findings reported in chapter five indicate that cropping intensity tends to differ across farms according to whether it operates under government owned and managed irrigation system or privately owned systems. To capture the effect of this factor, the sample farmers have been first divided into three categories, viz. (a) those operating under fully government and operated irrigation system, (b) those operating under government owned but with participation in and control over management and operation by farmers, and (c) those operating with self-owned STW based irrigation systems.

To capture the effect of levels of ownership and control of farmers over irrigation supply, the dummy variables I_b and I_c are incorporated in the econometric model. I_b takes the value 1 for farmers where the irrigation facility is owned by government but farmers have control over its management and operation and 0 for other categories. I_c takes the value 1 for farmers where the irrigation system is owned and operated by farmers and 0 for other situations. Thus the coefficients of I_b and I_c in the regression models will capture the differential effects for category (b) irrigation systems owned by government agencies but managed by stake-holding farmers and (c) fully owned and operated by the farmers respectively over category (a) which are fully owned and operated by government. A priory the coefficients of I_b and I_c are expected to take positive signs.

(b) Farm Size

Farm size has often been found to be an important factor influencing effective use of productivity raising farm practices associated with irrigation. However, the direction of the impact has been found to be varying from situation to situation (Bezbaruah, 1994). Cropping intensity is expected to be higher for smaller farms as smaller farms can be expected to use their limited land resource more intensively. Here the farm size is measured by operational holding of the farm in hectares and is denoted by the variable OH.

(c) Tenancy

The tenancy factor is measured by the percentage of leased in land in operational holding of the farm and is denoted by the variable T. *A priori* the tenancy factor can be expected to have a negative impact on cropping intensity.

(d) Extension

Better access to extension service is expected to help the farmers in adoption and use of better farming practices including multiple cropping. To measure this factor, the questionnaire used in the field study contained six questions related to a farmer's interactions with the extension agency. Farmers' responses to these queries were codified into scores. The total score on these questions could vary from 0 to 6 depending on the level of the farmer's interactions with the extension agencies. A farmer's score on these questions has been used as the measure of his access to extension service. (For details of the scoring refer Appendix 5.A). This variable representing farmers' access to extension service is denoted by E. As access to extension is likely to facilitate better farm practices, the coefficient of E should be positive.

(e) Location Factor

Since the field study was carried out in three districts located in three agro-climatic zones of the state, the difference in location of a sample farm can have some influence on the level of use of the different practices. Since there are three different locations, two dummies, namely L_1 and L_2 had to be taken to capture the effect of the locational factor. The dummy L_1 takes the value 1 for sample farms in Nagaon district and 0 for sample farms in the other two districts. Again, the dummy L_2 takes the value 1 for sample farms in Barpeta district and 0 for others. Thus the coefficient of L_1 captures the differential effect on the dependent variable for farms in Nagaon district over farms in Dibrugarh for which both L_1 and L_2 are zero. Similarly, coefficient of L_2 captures the differential effect on cropping intensity for farms in Barpeta district over farms in Dibrugarh.

(f) High Yielding Variety Seeds

Cropping intensity is also expected to be influenced by HYV_G, i.e. percentage of area under high yielding rice varieties in gross cropped area. The shorter duration of HYV crops can facilitate increased cropping intensity by releasing land quickly for another round of cultivation.

The linear regression model for explaining variation in cropping intensity in sample farms is thus formulated as —

$$CI = \alpha_0+\alpha_1 I_b+\alpha_2 I_c+\alpha_3 OH+\alpha_4 T+\alpha_5 E+\alpha_6 L_1+\alpha_7 L_2+\alpha_8 HYV_G+u \quad (7.1)$$

where u is the random disturbance term and the αs are the parameters to be estimated.

Estimated results of the regression equation (7.1) are presented in Table 7.1.

Table 7.1 : The Results of the Multiple Regression Analysis of Cropping Intensity in Sample Farms

Variable	*Estimated Coefficients*	*Standard Error of Coefficients*
(1)	*(2)*	*(3)*
Constant	150.323***	10.343
I_b	7.136	10.096
I_c	49.553***	8.132
OH	- 4.178**	1.871
T	0.097	0.126
E	3.160*	1.873
L_1	4.043	8.725
L_2	9.109	7.778
HYV_G	2.891	15.693
R^2	0.314	
$F(n_1=8,\ n_2=163)$	9.334 ***	

*,**,*** indicate significant at 0.10, 0.05 and 0.01 level respectively.

The apparently moderate R^2 value of 0.314 cannot be

dismissed as too small in the context of a detailed cross-sectional study as the present one. The fact that F-statistic for the overall regression model is statistically highly significant affirms the credibility of the results. Apart from the constant term, three out of the eight coefficients are also statistically significant.

The variable I_c is found to be statistically highly significant (significant at 1% level) with a positive coefficient though the variable I_b is not significant. This implies that the farms using private well based irrigation have a higher cropping intensity than farms depending on government irrigation supply. This finding is in conformity with the one observed by Mellor and Moorti (1971) who found privately owned tube-wells to be more efficient in achieving greater cropping intensity compared to government tube-wells in a study in Aligarh district of Uttar Pradesh. The result can be rationalized in terms of greater control over irrigation facility in case of private irrigation than in situations when the government is the supplier of the service. Fuller control gives the farmers freedom and flexibility of irrigating fields often enough for multiple cropping.

The other significant factor explaining cropping intensity is the farm size which is significant at 5 per cent level and access to extension services at 10 per cent level of significance. Farm size has a negative coefficient indicating that smaller farms use land with greater intensity. The obvious explanation is that availability of land being less, this resource is more intensively utilised. The coefficient of extension is expectedly positive showing that access to extension service induces farmers to adopt multiple cropping. All other factors in the model, viz. I_b, tenancy, HYV_G and both the locational dummies are found insignificant.

7.3 Analysis of Crop Diversification

Farmers contacted in the field study generally reported that they had been able to diversify the cropping pattern after having access to irrigation facility. In that context, it was considered worthwhile to examine whether extent of crop diversification varied significantly depending on the form of irrigation in which farmers operate. Crop diversification in the context of Assam can be interpreted in two ways—

1. Since traditionally the state is predominantly a rice growing area, the proportion of area under non-rice crops in the GCA can be taken as the measure of crop diversification. This proportion is denoted by the variable CD_r.
2. Not only is Assam a traditionally rice growing state, but in the rice acerage, the *kharif* winter rice crop has been the most dominant. Hence, the proportion of area under all non-winter rice crops in gross cropped area (GCA) can also be used as a measure of crop diversification. This proportion is denoted by the variable CD_w.

To explain the variation in crop diversification across sample farms, the same set of explanatory variables was used as in case of analysis of multiple cropping. However, the linear functional form was not found quite suitable for explaining this variation. The relevant dependent variable CD being contained in the range 0 to 1, a more appropriate functional form would be one in which the estimated value of the dependant variable will be contained within the range 0 and 1. Accordingly, the following logistic functional form was chosen :

$$CD = \frac{1}{1+e^{-z}} + u \qquad (7.2)$$

where $Z = \beta_0 + \beta_1 IF + \beta_2 FS + \beta_3 T + \beta_4 E + \beta_5 L_1 + \beta_6 L_2$ (7.3)

u is the random disturbance term and the βs are the parameters to be estimated.

It may be noted that as z goes from -α to α expected value of CD increases from 0 to 1.

The equation (7.2) has been estimated by non-linear least squares estimator method. The model is estimated twice by using the two alternative definitions of crop diversification as stated above. The estimated results using CD_r as the dependent variable are presented in Table 7.2 (a).

Table 7.2 (a) : The Results of Non-Linear Least Squares Estimation for Explaining Crop Diversification (CD_r) across Sample Farms

Variables	*Estimated Coefficients*	*Standard Error of Coefficients*
(1)	*(2)*	*(3)*
Constant	–1.720***	0.236
I_b	0.239	0.218
I_c	1.220***	0.214
OH	–0.009	0.049
T	0.007**	0.003
E	0.031	0.049
L_1	–0.835***	0.225
L_2	0.275	0.204
R^2	0.345	
F (n_1=7, n_2=164)	12.356***	

** *** indicate significant at 0.05 and 0.01 level respectively.

The model gives a fairly good fit to the sample data in terms of R^2 value (R^2 = 0.345). The F-statistic for overall regression is also highly statistically significant. Thus, on the whole, the results obtained from the analysis are fairly credible.

The variable I_c has come out statistically highly significant (at 1% level) with positive sign. This shows that farmers under privately owned shallow tube-wells tend to put more of their cropped area under non-rice crops than those operating under government owned schemes with and without participation in operation and management.

The coefficient of the variable T representing the tenancy factor is positive and significant. This phenomenon can be explained by the observed practice among sizeable number of sample farmers to take land on lease for growing vegetables with irrigation. Such tenancy, however, is different from usual share cropping as land in such cases is taken on lease on fixed rent. The positive and highly significant dummy variable L_1 shows that farmers in Nagaon district are able to diversify more to non-rice crops in their gross cropped area as compared to farmers in other two districts.

The estimated results using CD_w as the dependent variable are presented in Table 7.2 (b)

Table 7.2 (b) : The Results of Non-linear Least Squares Estimation for Explaining Variations in the Crop Diversification (CD) across Sample Farms

Variables	*Estimated Coefficients*	*Standard Error of Coefficients*
(1)	*(2)*	*(3)*
Constant	–.367	0.368
I_b	3.014***	0.339
I_c	2.389***	0.333
OH	–0.293***	0.076
T	0.005	0.005
E	–0.047	0.077
L_1	–1.403***	0.350
L_2	0.934***	0.318
R^2	0.467	
F (n_1=7, n_2=164)	20.506***	

*** indicates significant at 0.01 level.

The model gives a reasonably good fit to the sample data in terms of the R^2 value ($R^2 = 0.467$). The F-statistic for overall significance of the fitted regression has also been found to be statistically highly significant. Moreover, five out of the seven parameters of the function are found to be statistically significant showing the relevance of the corresponding factors in explaining the crop diversification in the sample farms. Thus, the results obtained from the analysis are credible.

It has been found that both the dummies for irrigation forms, i.e. I_b and I_c are highly significant (at 1% level) with positive coefficients. Thus farmers operating with private irrigation and those receiving irrigation from public sector projects but with control over operation and management of the supply put more of their cropped area under non-winter paddy crops than those depending on irrigation from government owned and operated projects.

The negative and significant coefficient of the variable OH indicates that the smaller farms actually put larger proportions of their cropped area under non-winter paddy crops.

The positive and statistically significant coefficients of the locational dummies indicate that farmers in Nagaon and Barpeta district put larger proportions of their cropped area under non-winter paddy crops than those in Dibrugarh.

The coefficient of tenancy factor (T) is found to be positive while coefficient of access to extension (E) is negative. However, none of them is statistically significant.

Thus, while examining the factors for variation in crop diversification across farms, different variables are found to have significant influence on the dependent variable. In case of crop diversification measured by proportion of non-rice crops in gross cropped area, the significant variables are the irrigation form represented by I_c, tenancy and the locational dummy for Nagaon over Dibrugarh. However, for crop diversification as defined by proportion of non-winter paddy crops in gross cropped area, besides irrigation form and locational dummies, the other significant variable is farm size. Thus, while tenancy is significant for the first type of crop diversification only, farm size is significant only for the second type of crop diversification. Irrigation form, however, is significant for both these types of crop diversification indicating that farmers in possession of private irrigation schemes and those under government irrigation schemes but with control in their operation have been more successful in crop diversification.

7.4 Analysis of Use of High Yielding Varieties

The analysis in chapter 5 reveals that adoption of high yielding paddy varieties is almost universal among the sample farmers. Yet, it has also been observed that the sample farmers taken together have not been able to extend the acreage under HYVs beyond 51 per cent of total area under paddy for private and 58 per cent for government irrigation schemes. Among the different sample farmers, of course, there has been extreme variation in the percentage of HYV area in the total area under paddy. It is, therefore, important to examine the conditions which encourage some farmers to use HYVs extensively and also those which hinder other farmers from doing the same. It is with this purpose a linear regression analysis was undertaken with percentage of HYV area in rice acerage as the dependent variable, denoted by HYV_R.

For analysing the variation of the dependent variable HYV_R across farms, the same set of factors, namely irrigation form, farm size, tenancy, access to extension and district locations, as in case of analysis of multiple cropping and crop diversification has been taken as explanatory factors.

Thus, the regression model chosen is –

$$HYV_R = \delta_0 + \delta_1 I_b + \delta_2 I_c + \delta_3 OH + \delta_4 T + \delta_5 E + \delta_6 L_1 + \delta_7 L_2 + u \tag{7.4}$$

where u is the random disturbance term and the δs are the parameters to be estimated.

The results of the regression analysis as estimated by the method of Ordinary Least Squares are shown in Table 7.3.

Table 7.3 : The Results of Multiple Regression Analysis of Variation in the Use of HYV Paddy across Sample Farms

Variables	*Estimated Coefficients*	*Standard Error of Coefficients*
(1)	*(2)*	*(3)*
Constant	35.785***	5.689
I_b	48.335***	5.240
I_c	8.521*	5.155
OH	-1.628	1.175
T	0.057	0.080
E	2.184*	1.186
L_1	10.036*	5.411
L_2	-1.790	4.917
R^2	0.441	
$F(n_1=7, n_2=164)$	18.487***	

* *** indicate significant at 0.10 and 0.01 level respectively.

The value of R^2, the coefficient of determination, is 0.441 which implies that the regression is a reasonably good fit. The F-statistic for overall regression is found highly significant. Again, four out of seven parameters have been found statistically significant showing the relevance of the corresponding factors in explaining the variation in the use of HYV paddy by the sample farmers. Thus, on the whole, the model is a fairly good fit to analyse the variation in use of HYVs by sample farmers.

It is clear from Table 7.3 that both the variables I_b and I_c are significant with positive coefficients. Thus farmers operating with private irrigation and those receiving irrigation from public sector projects but with control over operation and management of the supply use high yielding varieties more extensively than those depending on irrigation from government owned and operated projects. Indeed the variable I_b is more highly significant (at 1% level of significance) than I_c which is significant at 10 per cent level of significance and also has a larger coefficient. Thus in case of use of high yielding varieties the farmers using government irrigation but with control over operation and management do better than even the farmers operating with private irrigation. The other significant variables are the locational dummy L_1 and access to extension (E) both at 10 per cent level of significance. The positive and relatively highly significant coefficient of the dummy variable L_1 coupled with non-significance of the other locational dummy L_2 shows that farmers in Nagaon district in Central Brahmaputra Valley put a higher percentage of rice acreage under HYV compared to farmers in the other locations. The significance of E with a positive coefficient indicates that farmers with a closer contact with extension agencies tend to use HYVs more extensively. The other factors, namely, farm size (OH), tenancy (T) and the locational dummy L_2 are found insignificant.

7.5 Analysis of Use of Chemical Fertiliser

Use of chemical fertilizer has been measured by the amounts of N+P+K per hectare of gross cropped area of the farmer and is denoted by the variable FC. This dependent variable is regressed to the following factors —

(a) percentage of area under high yielding rice varieties in gross cropped area, denoted by HYV_G. It is expected that higher proportion of HYVs will induce use of nutrients in higher dose due to complementarities between the factors,
(b) irrigation forms as captured by the two dummy variables I_b and I_c,
(c) farm size measured by operational holding of the farm in hectares (OH),
(d) tenancy denoted by the variable T,
(e) access to extension service measured by variable E, and
(f) locational factor captured by the dummies L_1 and L_2.

A linear regression model of the following form has been formulated to see whether use of soil nutrients varies significantly across different forms :

$$FC = \chi_0 + \chi_1 I_b + \chi_2 I_c + \chi_3 OH + \chi_4 T + \chi_5 E + \chi_6 L_1 + \chi_7 L_2 + \chi_8 HYV_G + u \quad (7.5)$$

where u is the random disturbance term and the χs are the parameters to be estimated.

The Ordinary Least Squares estimates of the parameters of the model are presented in Table 7.4.

Table 7.4 : The Results of the Multiple Regression Analysis of Use of Chemical Fertiliser by Sample Farms

Variables	*Estimated Coefficients*	*Standard Error of Coefficients*
(1)	*(2)*	*(3)*
Constant	–14.104	16.436
I_b	102.652***	16.043
I_c	49.783***	12.923
OH	3.061	2.972
T	0.670***	0.200
E	2.327	2.976
L_1	10.727	13.864
L_2	29.041**	12.360
HYV_G	30.240	24.936
R^2	0.413	
F (n_1=8, n_2=163)	14.308***	

, * indicate significant at 0.05 and 0.01 respectively.

The R^2 value has come out to be 0.413 signifying explanatory powers of 41.3 per cent of the equation. The F-statistic for overall significance of the estimated equation has turned out to be statistically highly significant. Thus, the results of our regression analysis are found to be quite meaningful.

Both the variables I_b and I_c representing irrigation form are found to be statistically highly significant (significant at

1% level of significance) with positive coefficients. This shows that farmers using private irrigation as well as those using government irrigation but with control over operation and management of systems tend to use more fertilizer per hectare than the farmers depending on government owned and operated irrigation supply. The fact that coefficient of I_b is more than the double the size of coefficient of I_c shows that the farmers with government irrigation with control over operation and management do much better than the farmers operating with private irrigation in terms of use of fertilizer. Among other variables, tenancy (T) is found to be statistically highly significant (at 1 level of significance) indicating that tenant farmers have a tendency to use more fertilizers than those operating on their own. The statistically significant locational dummy L_2 (significant at 5% level of significance) indicates that farmers in Barpeta district use relatively more fertilizers than their counterparts in other locations. All other factors included in the model, namely farm size, extension, locational dummy L_1 and HYV_G are found insignificant.

7.6 Analysis of Yield of Rice

As reported in chapter 5, yield of rice in irrigated farms is found to be high in all the irrigation schemes. There is, however, variation in yield of the crop in different schemes. The yield per hectare has been recorded to have varied from 1612 kg to 4447 kg. This variation in the yield of rice among farms needs to be explained. Accordingly, a multiple regression analysis of yield of rice per hectare in sample farms, denoted by the variable HYV_R has been carried out. The explanatory factors taken for the purpose are –

(a) percentage of HYV in rice acerage, denoted by HYV_R. The variable is expected to have a positive impact on the indicator Y_R
(b) consumption of fertilizer measured by 'kilograms of N+P+K per hectare of rice acreage' denoted by F_R,

(c) irrigation form as captured by the dummy variables I_b and I_c,
(d) farm size measured by variable OH,
(e) tenancy measured by variable T,
(f) access to extension service measured by variable E, and
(g) locational factor captured by the dummies L_1 and L_2.

Thus the linear regression model used takes the following form :

$$Y_R=\Phi_0+\Phi_1 I_b+\Phi_2 I_c+\Phi_3 OH+\Phi_4 T+\Phi_5 E+\Phi_6 L_1+\Phi_7 L_2+\Phi_8 HYV_R+\Phi_9 F_R+u \quad (7.6)$$

where u is the random disturbance term and Φs are the parameters to be estimated.

The coefficients of the variables are estimated by using the method of Ordinary Least Squares (OLS). The results of the regression analysis are presented in Table 7.5.

Table 7.5 : The Results of the Multiple Regression Analysis of Yield of Rice across Farms

Variables	*Estimated Coefficients*	*Standard Error of Coefficients*
(1)	*(2)*	*(3)*
Constant	15.577***	1.318
I_b	5.320***	1.386
I_c	1.489	1.161
OH	0.562**	0.239
HYV_R	0.094***	0.016
F_R	0.033***	0.007
T	–0.016	0.016
E	–0.071	0.243
L_1	–0.161	1.108
L_2	–0.868	1.079
R^2	0.631	
$F(n_1=9, n_2=162)$	30.762***	

, * indicate significant at 0.05 and 0.01 level respectively.

The model gives a good fit to the sample data in terms of R^2 value of 0.631. The F-statistic for overall significance of the fitted regression is statistically highly significant. Moreover, four out of the nine parameters of the function have come statistically significant.

In case of yield of rice too, the coefficients of the variables I_b and I_c are positive. However, while the variable I_b is statistically highly significant (at 1% level of significance), I_c is not found significant. Thus farmers operating under government irrigation with control over operation and management are able to extract higher yield from their principal crop, rice than the other two categories of farmers. This is to be expected as this category of farmers has been found to be using high yielding varieties and fertilizers to greater extent than the other two categories.

Among the other factors, farm size represented by the variable OH is found to be significant at 5 per cent level of significance. From the significant and positive coefficient of OH it can be inferred that cultivators with larger farm size tend to have higher rate of yield of rice per hectare. This finding is in conformity with the results obtained by Singh and Kalra (2002) in a study related to production of rice in Punjab. They found that yield of rice had positive association with farm size, the large farms having yields higher than the smaller ones.

Among the other variables, HYV_R and F_R are expectedly highly significant (at 1% level of significance) with positive coefficients. The positive and highly significant coefficient of HYV_R implies that larger proportion of rice acerage under high yielding variety tends to raise the yield of the crop. The positive and significant coefficient of the variable F_R indicates that higher the amount of soil nutrients applied per hectare of rice acerage, the higher will be the yield of rice.

All other variables included in the model, namely I_c, tenancy, extension and the locational dummies L_1 and L_2 are found insignificant.

7.7 Conclusion

It is clear from above analysis that farmers in category (b) and (c), i. e. those using water from private irrigation systems and from government irrigation schemes but with participation of stake-holding farmers in control and management, have been able to use irrigation more effectively than those in category (a), i.e. irrigation schemes owned and operated by the government. The results of econometric models confirm that on the whole farmers operating under government supplied irrigation but with control over operation and management of the systems and farmers operating with private irrigation use irrigation water more effectively than those operating under government owned and operated irrigation systems.

There are, however, significant differences between farmers operating under government irrigation with control in operation and management and farmers operating with tube-well based private irrigation in the use of practices, levels of which are taken as indicators of effective use of irrigation. The former category of farmers has utilized HYV seeds-fertilizer technology of foodgrain production in a fuller way and hence achieved higher yield of rice. The latter group, on the other hand, has achieved higher cropping intensity and higher crop diversification. It seems that fuller control over irrigation supply from small scale and mostly self-owned tube-well based systems give farmers in this category more flexibility in choosing crops and crop seasons, enabling more frequent cropping of their fields. Indeed these farmers have been found to have diversified to non-rice crops to a greater extent than farmers operating with government supplied irrigation with or without control over operation and management of supply.

Among the other institutional factors, while farm size is found to have significant influence on the indicators of cropping intensity, crop diversification and yield of rice, tenancy is found significant in crop diversification and use of fertilizers. The locational dummies are found significant in case of crop diversification, extent of HYV seeds (L_1) and use of fertilizers (L_2). The factor access to extension is found significant in explaining the indicators, viz. cropping intensity and extent of use of HYV seeds. Among the other factors, percentage of HYV area in total rice acerage and kilograms of N+P+K fertilizer use per hectare of rice (F_R) are expectedly found positive and significant in explaining the indicator, yield of principal crop, rice.

Thus, participation of stake-holding farmers in control and management of government owned irrigation systems has been found to be a significant factor in inducing and enabling farmers to use productivity raising practices and inputs at a higher level. In situations where farmers' associations are involved in management and operation of government schemes and better coordination between supplier and users of irrigation is accordingly achieved, farmers have been found to use productivity raising practices at a higher level.

NOTE

1. Field Management Committee (FMC) also known as *Pathar Parichalana Samiti* is a peer organisation of farmers in a village. The initial idea behind formation of this *Samiti* was to have better coordination among farmers operating in the same field so as to facilitate the spread of better farming practices. Though the idea of this *Samiti* was mooted way back in early 1960s, the *Samitis* came to be active in pockets only since the late 1980s. In the recent past *Samitis* have been formed all over the state with active facilitation by government extension agencies.

REFERENCES

Bezbaruah, M. P. (1994), *Technological Transformation of Agriculture : A Study from Assam*, Mittal Publications, New Delhi.

Mellor, John W. and Moorti, T. V. (1971), "Dilemma of State Tube Wells", *Economic and Political Weekly*, Vol. 3, No. 6, March 27.

Singh, K. and Kalra, S. (2002), "Rice Production in Punjab : Systems, Varietal Diversity, Growth and Sustainability", *Economic and Political Weekly*, p. 3139, July 27.

8

Summary of Findings, Conclusion and Policy Suggestions

Before drawing the final conclusion and working out the policy implications, it may be worthwhile to go over the principal findings of the study. A summary of these findings is presented in the following section.

8.1 Principal Findings

- As against the ultimate irrigation potential of 27 lakh hectares in the state, irrigation potential of only 10,32,830 hectares has been created till the end of 2001-02. In other words, only 38.25 per cent of ultimate irrigation potential of the state has been realised so far. Schemewise, major and medium schemes have accounted for 19.59 per cent of the total potential created while the rest 80.41 per cent is created under minor schemes.
- Utilisation of the potential created is not found to be satisfactory. Up to the end of 2000-01, utilisation of potential created under government sector comes out to be as low as 22.96 per cent. This utilisation rate is not only low but is also decreasing over the years. Thus there has been gross underutilisation of irrigation potential created in the state.

- Sharp variation is noticed in the rates of utilisation in the two types of irrigation schemes. The estimated utilisation rate for government irrigation schemes was found to be 34.24 per cent whereas the same for private schemes was 51.92 per cent. Thus, the performance of private irrigation schemes is found to be better in so far as utilisation of created potential is concerned. Difference in utilisation rate, however, is noticed in case of privately owned schemes as well depending upon the location to which the scheme belongs. Thus utilisation rate is found to be best in Barpeta (66.06%) followed by Dibrugarh (43.42%) and Nagaon (40.40%). The highest utilisation rate in case of government irrigation schemes is observed in Jamuna Irrigation Scheme (66.92%) followed by Chenga (42.5%), Puthimari (41.25%), Duliabam (39.29%) and Mandia (30.5%).
- Variation is also observed in the availability of irrigation water in the field depending on the type of irrigation scheme under which the farm operates. On the whole, 61 per cent of the sample farmers under government schemes received water as per their requirements, whereas 82 per cent of the farmers operating under private schemes received the same. Clearly, the performance of the privately owned shallow tube-well schemes has been superior to that of government owned schemes in so far as providing water according to the requirements of the farmers is concerned.

Even within government sector, under the major and medium schemes sharp variations in water availability in different reaches of the command area were observed. For instance, in case of the major irrigation project of Jamuna, the irrigated area per hectare of operational holding in middle reach was found to be 1.41 whereas the same in the tail reach was as low as 0.48. In case of government minor schemes such variations were not pronounced.

- The factors identified for underutilisation of irrigation potential created under government owned schemes have been found to be largely supply side related. The main factor responsible for poor utilisation of government owned irrigation schemes is lack of maintenance. Maintenance work has suffered because the government agencies do not have the funds for carrying out such works. While maintenance operation suffers because of lack of funds, the practice of collection of water charge from beneficiary farmers is absent in all the government schemes. In fact, the practice of collecting water levy was stopped for political reasons in late 1970s and has not been revived ever since.

Low utilisation of irrigation potential is also due to lack of coordination between various agencies such as different wings of Irrigation Department, State Electricity Board, etc. involved in delivering irrigation water to the field. In case of lift irrigation schemes, lack of coordination between Irrigation Department and Electricity Board is one of the major problems. These factors, afflicting the efficiency of utilisation of government owned schemes, can be categorised under management and administration related problems.

Faulty design of canals is also found to create problems in achieving fuller utilisation of irrigation potential in certain parts of command areas of a number of irrigation schemes.
In certain parts of the command areas of some of the schemes, the necessary land levelling has not been carried out or completed. Consequently, these parts have not received irrigation water as projected in the initial project report.

- Even in those government owned schemes in which the coordination between the Irrigation Department and the farming community is better and farmers' associations like the Field Management Committees (FMCs) are involved in management, utilisation rate is appreciably better.

- The privately owned shallow tube-well (STW) schemes are generally free from the supply side factors afflicting the government schemes which explains the better utilisation rates observed in case of the former. In other words, the better performance of private minor schemes in supplying irrigation water to fields can be attributed mainly to a better maintenance and management of these schemes. However, the utilisation rate of 51.92 per cent of private sector schemes can also do with considerable improvement. The utilisation rate of these schemes is found to be constrained by small and fragmentation of holdings. However, emergence of groundwater market in certain areas has facilitated the owners of STWs to sell water to the neighbouring farmers. This development is found to have helped in better utilisation of irrigation potential in spite of predominance of small and fragmented holdings.

- While no definite pattern can be noticed regarding cropwise irrigation under government schemes, a clear and definite pattern is observed in case of privately owned schemes in use of irrigation water under different crops. In case of private schemes irrigation is utilised to a greater extent for non-rice crops in general and non-winter paddy crops in particular than under government schemes. This indicates that private irrigation may have facilitated the crop diversification more than government irrigation schemes.

- The average cropping intensity of the sample farmers under private irrigation is found to be higher than those under government irrigation. The multiple regression analysis also confirms that intensity of cropping tends to be higher for farms operating with private irrigation than for farms operating with government provided irrigation. Apart from the difference in ownership of the irrigation schemes, farm size and access to extension service have been found to significantly influence cropping intensity. The cropping intensity has been found to be negatively associated with the size of operational holding indicating that, a small farmer tends to use his cultivable land more intensively than a farmer with large operational holdings. On the other hand, better access to extension has been found to facilitate greater cropping intensity.
- Availability of irrigation in general has been found to help diversification of cropping pattern. But in this context also the farmers operating with privately owned schemes (non-rice crops) and farmers operating with private irrigation and those receiving irrigation from public sector projects but with control over operation and management of the supply (non-winter paddy crop) have achieved greater diversification than farms operating under government owned schemes.
- The average rate of fertilizer consumption in sample farms has been found to be 93.22 kg. of N, P, K per hectare which is about five times the rate for the state as a whole. This sample average is comparable to the rates of fertilizer consumption in states like Uttar Pradesh, West Bengal, etc. which are agriculturally more advanced than Assam. This shows that with availability of irrigation, farmers in Assam too tend

to use productivity raising inputs more abundantly. However, as in the case of crop diversification (non-winter paddy crop in the GCA) farmers using private irrigation as well as those using government irrigation but with control over operation and management of systems tend to use more fertilizer per hectare than the farmers depending on government owned and operated irrigation supply. Apart from ownership of irrigation, the factor significantly influencing use of fertilizer in sample farms is tenancy with positive coefficients. The positive relation of fertilizer use to tenancy is theoretically contrary to expectations. This apparently counter intuitive phenomenon can be explained by tendency among a section of sample farmers to take land on lease for cultivation of vegetables with irrigation.

- In case of use of high yielding varieties, the farmers using government irrigation but with control over operation and management and those using private irrigation are found to perform better than those under government irrigation. However, the former category farmers are found to do much better than even the latter category of farmers.
- In case of attainment of yield of rice again, farmers operating under government irrigation with control over operation and management are found to extract higher yield from their principal crop, rice than the other two categories of farmers. This is to be expected as this category of farmers has been found to be using high yielding varieties and fertilizers to greater extent than the other two categories.

The findings clearly show that the efficiency in utilisation of created irrigation potential and effectiveness of irrigation in enabling farmers in using better farming practices and achieving higher performance level differ significantly depending on the form and type of irrigation under which farmers operate. In particular, privately owned irrigation schemes are more efficient in utilisation of irrigation capacity and effective in inducing and enabling farmers in using better farming practices than government owned and operated schemes. Within government schemes, the efficiency and effectiveness have been found to be better in situations where the farmers' associations have a significant role in management of the schemes and consequently a greater coordination between government irrigation department and water using farmers takes place.

8.2 Conclusion

Since about half of the irrigation potential created in the state is under government owned schemes, it is the relatively poorer utilisation of irrigation potential of such government owned schemes which pulls down the overall utilisation rate of irrigation in the state. As inefficient management has been identified from the study as the principal cause of lower utilisation rate of the government owned schemes the hypothesis that inefficient management of government owned and operated irrigation schemes is responsible for dismal utilisation rate of created irrigation potential in the state gets accepted.

The evidence from the field study does not provide general support to the hypothesis that faulty design has resulted in low utilisation of capacity of the projects. However, for certain limited parts of command areas under government operated schemes, faulty designing of canal structure has been found to cause problems in supplying water to the fields. Thus, the hypothesis that faulty design has resulted in low utilisation of capacity of the projects is valid only for some specific areas but not valid for irrigation schemes in the state in general.

The hypothesis that low utilisation in irrigation projects of the state is due to absence of land reform and preparation measures has been found to be true in two contexts. In some of the government schemes due to absence of proper land levelling and preparation works, portions of command area could never get water from the project. This has contributed to lowering of the utilisation of the created potential as per initial project report. The hypothesis also seems to be valid for some instances of low utilisation rates under private schemes in situations where relatively smaller and fragmented holdings are more common. In some such areas, however, emergence of water market seems to be facilitating fuller utilisation of capacity in spite of holding fragmentation. The emerging groundwater market has thus, appeared to be functioning as a substitute of consolidation of holdings at least for fuller utilisation of irrigation capacity.

8.3 Policy Suggestions

The main policy suggestions emerging from the findings of the study are summed up in the following paragraphs :

(i) Irrigation potential which is already created under government sector should ensure better returns. This can be done by improving the management aspects of the schemes. For this following measures can be taken up—

   (a) Collection of water charge from the beneficiary farmers, and
   (b) Involvement of farmers in management and operation of the schemes.

   Since lack of fund allocation is a main factor hampering maintenance work, collection of water levy can generate the necessary fund for maintenance and operation. Therefore, the practice of collecting water levy should be revived. Collections from water levy should be kept separately so that the necessary fund can be made available as and when required for maintenance operation. This will ensure that maintenance activity will not be held up by usual bureaucratic procedures of sanctioning and releasing fund from the general government fund.

Since participation of farmers in management ensures better control of water distribution to the field resulting in better utilisation of potential created and effectiveness, the involvement of stake-holding farmers in operation and management of irrigation systems should be secured wherever possible. In this context, Rao (2002) in a paper called for greater involvement of the farmers' bodies like Water Users' Associations (WUA) in management of irrigation schemes. However, to be able to get involved effectively, farmers need to have the necessary peer organization among them. In situations where such peer organizations among farmers are weak or absent, it is necessary to facilitate emergence of such bodies in a robust manner.

(ii) The emergence of groundwater market should be facilitated as such development can ensure better utilisation of irrigation capacity of shallow tube-well based schemes in spite of the problems arising because of small and fragmented holdings. However, the process should be suitably regulated to prevent the growth of monopolistic tendency and over and unsustainable exploitation of the open access common property resource of groundwater reserve.

(iii) In view of higher efficiency in utilisation of irrigation potential and effectiveness in using better farming practices of small scale privately owned shallow tube-well based small-scale irrigation systems over government owned and operated major, medium and even minor irrigation schemes and the ground level conditions in the Brahmaputra Valley in the form of relatively small size of holdings and abundance of groundwater reserve, private investments in such systems can be encouraged so as to add to the total irrigation capacity. A larger share of the small scale private shallow tube-well irrigation in the total irrigation capacity should in itself lead to an improvement in the overall utilisation rate. In view of relative ease of managing and maintaining small-scale irrigation schemes, a number of studies have advocated for these schemes over large-scale irrigation projects in India (Puttaswamaiah,1977; Gogoi, 1989). However, unrestricted exploitation of the common resource of groundwater reserve may be unsustainable in the long term. Thus as the installation of tube-well based irrigation systems picks up, it will be necessary to put suitable regulations in place to ensure sustainable exploitation of the groundwater reserves. The regulations to avoid these problems may be in the form of specification of the size of the pump, in the number of pumps one can possess or specifying the density of STW based irrigation project in a specified area. (For example, one may not be allowed to install a very large capacity pump or a person already possessing a pump should not be allowed to have the second on subsidy). Indeed some regulations on paper have already come into existence. It has been observed that as per Agriculture Department, Government of Assam guidelines, an STW cannot be installed within 200 metres of another STW. However, enforcement of this regulation was not found in practice. It is, therefore, an imperative to set up mechanism for implementation of regulation with in-built system of taking into account the concerns of the community of farmers, the village community at large and the government agencies.

Development of groundwater based irrigation schemes will help in better utilisation of abundant groundwater resource of which only about 7 per cent is reported to be annually utilised at present in the state. The apprehension of groundwater depletion and resulting unsustainability of groundwater based irrigation systems is unwarranted in the context of Assam according to the Central Ground Water Board source. As the state falls in a high rainfall zone, there is every possibility of groundwater reserve being adequately replenished because of heavy monsoon precipitation in the region.

(iv) Development of groundwater based schemes, however, may not be possible in all the parts of the state due to specific geographical and geological conditions. For example, Barak Valley region of the state is poorly endowed with groundwater resource and the Hills are not suitable for development of groundwater based irrigation. Therefore, irrigation development in such areas has to be based on utilisation of available surface water resource such as river flow.

Development of surface water based schemes will generally require comparatively larger initial investment and will have to be operated at a bigger scale than the groundwater based shallow tube-well schemes. So, the farmers individually cannot be expected to develop such irrigation facilities. Government intervention will be necessary to directly invest in establishing irrigation capacity or facilitating farmers' groups to take up and deploy the necessary investment. Even if such irrigation capacity is installed under government sector, the government has to ensure a built-in mechanism for involvement of stake-holding farmers in the operation and management of the schemes from day one onwards so as to ensure their better efficiency and effectiveness.

REFERENCES

Gogoi, K. (1989), "Irrigation in Assam" in P. C. Goswami (Ed.) (1989), *Agriculture in Assam*, Assam Institute of Development Studies, Guwahati.

Puttaswamaiah, K. (1977), *Irrigation Projects in India—Towards a New Policy*, Nrusimha Publications, Bangalore.

Rao, C.H. Hanumantha (2002), "Sustainable Use of Water for Irrigation in Indian Agriculture", *Economic and Political Weekly*, May 4.

Bibliography

Alagh, Y. K. (1987), *The Next Phase of Water Planning*, Inaugural Address at the First National Water Convention held in Delhi, November 12.

Ali, A. N. M. Irshad (1975), *A Study on the Impact of Mayong Lift Irrigation Project*, Agro-Economic Research Centre for North East, Jorhat.

Appu, P. S. (1974), "The Bamboo Tubewell : A Low Cost Device for Exploiting Ground Water", *Economic and Political Weekly*, Vol. 26, p. A-63.

Assam Agricultural University (1990), *Report on the Survey of Iron Toxicity Problems of Ground Water in Crop Production in Assam*, AAU, Jorhat.

Bezbaruah, M. P. (1994), *Technological Transformation of Agriculture—A Study from Assam*, Mittal Publications, New Delhi.

Bhingraj, S. M. (1987), "Underutilisation of Irrigation Resources in India", *Commerce*, Vol. 154, No. 3959, April 4-10.

Burt, Charles M. (2007), *"Volumetric Irrigation Water Pricing Considerations"*, Irrigation and Drainage Systems, 21.1, 133-144 (http://works.bepress.com/cburt/56/) acces-sed on 6-8-2009.

Centre for Monitoring Indian Economy Pvt. Ltd. (2007), *Economic Intelligence Service : Agriculture*, April, Mumbai.

Chambers, Robert (1992), *Managing Canal Irrigation–Practical Analysis for South Asia*, Oxford and IBH Publishing Company Private Limited, New Delhi.

Chatterjee, Nandini (1995), *Irrigated Agriculture*, Rawat Publishers, Jaipur and New Delhi.

Choudhury, B. K. (1971), *Economics of Tube-Well Irrigation in West Bengal*, Agro-Economic Research Centre, Viswabharati.

Clark, Colin (1970), *The Economics of Irrigation* (2nd edition), ELBS and Pergamon Press, Oxford.

Cornish, G., et al (2004), *Water Charging in Irrigated Agriculture : An analysis of International Experience*, Food and Agriculture Organization of the United Nations (http://www.fao.org/docrep/008/y5690e/y5690e07.htm) accessed on 6-8-2009.

Das, Manmohan (1984), *Peasant Agriculture in Assam*, Inter India, New Delhi.

Dhawan, B. D. (1980), "Under utilisation of Groundwater Resources : A Case Study of East U. P.", *Economic and Political Weekly*, No. 39.

Dhawan, B. D. (1982), *Development of Tube-Well Irrigation in India*, Agricole Publishing Academy, New Delhi.

Dhawan, B. D.(1986), "Irrigation and Water Management in India : Perception of Problems and their Resolution", *Indian Journal of Agricultural Economics*, Vol. 41, No. 3, July-September.

Dhawan, B. D. and Dutta, H. S. (1992), "Impact of Irrigation on Multiple Cropping", *Economic and Political Weekly*, March 28.

Dhawan, B. D.(1995), "Magnitude of Ground water Exploitation", *Economic and Political Weekly*, April 8.

Dhawan, B. D. (1996), *Irrigation in India's Agricultural Development*, Sage Publications, New Delhi.

Dhawan, B. D. (1997), *India's Irrigation Sector—Myths and Realities*, Presidential Address of 57th Annual Conference of the Indian Society of Agricultural Economics held at G.B. Pant University of Agriculture and Technology, Pantnagar (mimeo).

Dutta, K. S. and Chang-Bao-Wen (1986), "Under utilisation of Canal Irrigation in Sona Command Area of Bihar", *Agricultural Situation in India*, Vol. XLI, No. 8.

Easter, K. W. (1974), "Improving Village Irrigation System : An Example for India", *Land Economics*, Vol. 53, No.1.

Fujita, K. and Hossain, F. (1995), " Role of the Groundwater Market in Agricultural Development and Income Distribution : A Case Study in North-West Bangladesh Village", *The Developing Economics*, XXXII-4.

Gadgil, D. R. (1948), *Economic Effects of Irrigation – Report of*

Survey of the Direct and Indirect Benefits of Godavari and Pravara Canals, Gokhale Institute of Politics and Economics, Pune.

Gogoi, Bharati (1993), "Irrigation and Agricultural Development in Assam" in K. Alam (1993) (ed.) *Agricultural Development in North-East India : Constraints and Prospects*, Deep and Deep Publcations, New Delhi.

Gogoi, K. (1989), "Irrigation in Assam" in P. C. Goswami (Ed.)(1989), *Agriculture in Assam*, Assam Institute of Development Studies, Guwahati.

Gohain, D. and Gogoi, K. (1986), *Problems of Underutilisation of Irrigation Potentials*, Agro Economic Research Centre for N.E. India, Jorhat (Mimeographed).

Goswami, A. (1992), "Some Constraints of Economic Development of Assam" in Saikia, P. D. and Borah, Durgeswar (Eds.) *Constraints of Economic Development in N. E. India*, Omsons Publications, New Delhi and Guwahati.

Goswami, D. C. (1989), "Floods and Their Impact on Agriculture in Assam" in Goswami, P. C. (ed.) *Agriculture in Assam*, Assam Institute of Development Studies, Guwahati.

Government of Assam (2002), *Economic Survey*, Directorate of Economics and Statistics, Guwahati-781006, Assam.

Government of Assam (2002), *Statistical Hand Book of Assam*, Directorate of Economics and Statistics, Guwahati-781006, Assam.

Government of India (1966), *Evaluation of Major Irrigation Projects—Some Case Studies*, Programme Evaluation Organisation, Planning Commission.

Government of India (1976), *Report of the National Commission on Agriculture*, Part V, p. 20

Government of India (1995), *Annual Report*, Ministry of Water Resources, Government of India.

Hardin, Garrett (1968), "The Tragedy of Commons", *Science*, 162 (Reprinted in Sankar, U. (Ed.) *Environmental Economics* (2001), Oxford University Press.

ICAR (1972), *Proceedings of the Symposium on Cropping Pattern in India*, Indian Council of Agricultural Research, p. 15.

Jha, U. M. (1984), *Irrigation and Agricultural Development*, Deep and Deep Publications, New Delhi.

Mellor, John W. and Moorti, T. V. (1971), " Dilemma of State Tube Wells", *Economic and Political Weekly*, Vol. 3, No. 6, March 27.

Mitra, A. K. (1984a), "Irrigation Sector Reforms—Issues and Approaches", *Economic and Political Weekly*, March 30.

Mitra, Ashok K. (1984b), "Managing Irrigation System in Drought Prone Areas", *Indian Journal of Agricultural Economics*, Vol. 39, No. 3, July-September.

Mitra, Ashok K. (1987), *Planning and Management of Surface Irrigation in Drought Prone Areas*, Gokhale Institute of Politics and Economics, Pune.

Mitra, Ashok K. (1991), "Water Resource Management—Discussion at Agricultural Economics Conference", *Economic and Political Weekly*, Review of Agriculture, September 28, p. A-115.

Narayanamoorthy, A. (1996), "Electric Pumpset and Groundwater Management—Macro and Micro Evidence of India", *Water Resources Journal*, June.

Palanisami, K. (1984), *Irrigation Water Management—the Determinants of Canal Water Distribution in India—A Micro Analysis*, Agricole Publishing Academy, New Delhi.

Pant, Niranjan (1981), *Some Aspects of Irrigation Administration : A Case Study of Kosi Project (Bihar)*, Naya Prakashan, Calcutta.

Pant, Niranjan (1991), "Groundwater Issues in Eastern India" in Ruth Meinzen-Dick and Mark Svendsen (ed.)(1991), *Future Directions for Indian Irrigation – Research and Policy Issues*, International Food Policy Research Institute, Washington D.C.

Patel, S. A. and Patel, H. F. (1983), "Irrigation Practices and Efficiency of Water Use—A study of Machchu 1 Irrigation Project Area in Gujarat", *Agricultural Situation in India*, p. 12, October.

Pawar, Chandrakanth T. (1989), *Impact of Irrigation : A Regional Perspective*, Himalaya Publishing House, Bombay.

Phukan, Umananda (1985), *A Study on the Impact of Deep Tubewell Irrigation on Crop Production in Jorhat District of Assam*, Agro Economic Research Centre for North-East India, Assam Agricultural University, Jorhat.

Phukan, Umananda (1986), *A Study on the Impact of Deep Tube-*

well Irrigation on Crop Production in Kamrup District of Assam, Agro Economic Research Centre for North-East India, Assam Agricultural University, Jorhat.

Puttaswamaiah, K. (1977), *Irrigation Projects in India— Towards a New Policy*, Nrusimha Publications, Bangalore.

Rao, C. H. H., Ray, S. K. and Subbarao, K. (1988), *Unstable Agriculture and Drought*, Vikash, New Delhi.

Rao, C. H. Hanumantha (2002), "Sustainable Use of Water for Irrigation in Indian Agriculture", *Economic and Political Weekly*, May 4.

Reddy, P. Sanjeeva (1997), *Different Sources of Irrigation*, Manak Publications Private Limited, New Delhi.

Roy, Niranjan and Bezbaruah, M. P. (2002), *Agricultural Growth and Regional Economic Development*, Mittal Publications, New Delhi.

Saikia, T. N. and Bora, D. R. (1993), *Economic Appraisal of CAD Programmes under Jamuna Irrigation Project in Assam (Part I)*, Agro Economic Research Centre for North-East India, Assam Agricultural University, Jorhat.

Satpathy, T. (1984), *Irrigation and Economic Development*, Asish Publishing House, New Delhi.

Satya Sai, K. J. S. (1990), "Impact of Irrigation on Intensity of Land Utilisation" in Tyagi, N. K., Joshi, P. K. and Singh, N. T. (ed.) *National Symposium on Management of Irrigation System*, Central Soil Salinity Research Institute, Karnal.

Satyasai, K. J. S., Kumar Praduman and Mruthyunjaya (1997), "Terms of Transactions in Groundwater Markets : A Study in Anantapur District of Andhra Pradesh", *Indian Journal of Agricultural Economics*, Vol. 52, No. 4, October-December.

Sawant, S.D. (1986), "Irrigation and Water Use" in Indian Society of Agricultural Economics (1986) *Indian Agricultural Development Since Independence*, Oxford & IBH.

Shah, Tushaar and K. Vengama Raju (1987), "Working of Groundwater Market in Andhra Pradesh and Gujarat : Results of two Village Studies", *Economic and Political Weekly*, Vol. 22, No. 13, March 26.

Sharma, P. (1992), *A Study of Irrigation Development and Its Impact on Foodgrains Production in Assam*, Ph.D. Thesis, Gauhati University.

Singh, Baldev (1991), "Impact of Irrigation on Income, Employment and Land Use Pattern in Punjab", *Indian Journal of Agricultural Economics*, Vol. XLVI, No. 4.

Singh, K. and Kalra, S. (2002), "Rice Production in Punjab : Systems, Varietal Diversity, Growth and Sustainability", *Economic and Political Weekly*, p. 3139, July 27.

Srinivasmurthy, A.P. (1990), *Irrigation Planning in India*, Himalaya Publishing House, Bombay.

Stern, P. H. (1979), *Small Scale Irrigation*, Intermediate Technology Publications, London, U.K.

Sukla, L. and Gurjar, R. K. (1990), *Canal Irrigation Management*, Agricole Publishing Academy, New Delhi.

Swaminathan, M. S. (1981), *Irrigation and Our Agricultural Future*, First Ajudhia Nath Khosla Lecture, delivered at the University of Roorkee, Reproduced by Centre for Monitoring Indian Economy, Mumbai.

Vaidyanathan, A. (1996), "Depletion of Groundwater Exploitation : Some Issues", *Indian Journal of Agricultural Economics*, Vol. 51, No.1 and 2, January-June.

Venkataramani, G. (1974), *Minor Irrigation in Tamil Nadu*, Sangam Publishers, Madras for Madras Institute of Development Studies (MIDS).

Wade, Robert (1976), Performance of Irrigation Projects, *Economic and Political Weekly*, January 17, p. 64.

Wade, Robert (1978), "Water Supply as an Instrument of Agricultural Policy — A Case Study", *Economic and Political Weekly*, March 25.

Yousuf, Mohammed (1990), *Irrigation : Plan, Practice, Perspective*, Ajanta Publications, Delhi.

Index